DOLLARS FOR SCHOLARS

Everything You Need to Know about
Writing Essays that Win Scholarships,
the Scholarship Process,
and the Transition from High School
Senior to College Freshman

JOAQUÍN ZIHUATANEJO

cooLbooks

Dollars For Scholars
By Joaquín Zihuatanejo

Proofreading by Sarina Sarina Cornthwaite
Cover Conceptualization by Carlos Ojeda Jr.
Portrait photography by Jessica Ewald
Copy Editing, Cover Design & Layout Design by Iske Conradie

ISBN: 978-0-578-61637-7

For all of those scholars from the barrio or the fields

who dream of a way out

and a way back in

to create change.

"If I could go back, I'd coach myself. I'd be the woman who taught me how to stand up, how to want things, how to ask for them. I'd be the woman who says, your mind, your imagination, they are everything. Look how beautiful. You deserve to sit at the table. The radiance falls on all of us."

—Lidia Yuknavitch, from *The Chronology of Water*

TABLE OF CONTENTS

WHY DO I CALL YOU SCHOLARS INSTEAD OF STUDENTS?

This is an excellent question, and yet I can't quite remember which professor during my undergrad at college said this to us. I'm sure she may have heard it or read it from another source (and yes, I've added a bit of myself to this) but it has always stayed with me. I hope it stays with you.

STUDENTS are sometimes tardy and occasionally absent.

SCHOLARS are never tardy and rarely absent.

STUDENTS sit at the back of classroom with friends who may be a distraction to them and the classroom.

SCHOLARS sit at the front of the classroom away from anyone or anything that will be a hindrance to their learning process.

(This may seem unimportant in middle school or high school, but at university you may find yourself in a lecture hall with 325 other students. If you sit in the back of the classroom, arrive late occasionally, never raise your hand to ask a question, never introduce yourself to the professor, and never visit the professor during their Office Hours, and you are sitting at a 68.9% average at the end of the semester, do you think they will bump your grade to a 70%? The answer is likely, no. However, if you arrive early on the first day and introduce yourself to the professor, and sit in the front row, and ask pertinent questions, visit them and take advantage of Office Hours when you need help, that professor will get to know you throughout the semester as a human with a voice, and a face, and an unusual laugh. When you find yourself sitting at a 69.1% at the end of the semester, do you think they will bump your grade to a 70%? One cannot say for certain, but the odds are much better of your professor saying, yes. In this scenario the answer is maybe, but I'll take a maybe over a no any day of the week.)

A New Chapter

Time to do something

Scholar Hacks

Helpful Websites & Apps

Helpful Books

STUDENTS occasionally need to borrow a pen or paper or materials from someone else.

SCHOLARS keep a back-up to their back-up pen or pencil on their person and always arrive prepared to class.

STUDENTS take classes they know they can handle with relative ease.

SCHOLARS take classes they know will challenge them, even if it means sacrificing a high A in an easy class for a low A, or even a high B in a more challenging class.

A STUDENT thinks it all ends once they have earned their PhD. Now, they will never have to waste another second of their life learning.

A SCHOLAR thinks of learning as a life-long endeavor and yearns to learn the way one aches to sing, or dance, or play basketball, or whatever else you are desperate to do.

THE GOAL

I want you to walk away from this book *inspired*.

I want you to *gain knowledge* about what goes into writing a winning scholarship essay.

I want you to come to trust me as a teacher, and *grow as a writer* and a scholar from not only my expertise and victories but also *from my struggles and failures*. Yes... even teachers fail sometimes.

I want you to *have answers* to your questions.

I want you to know that **college is an opportunity open to everyone**.

I want you to know that you have a story to tell, and that there is **only one voice out there that sounds like yours**—that is an extraordinary fact.

I want you to **use that powerful voice of yours** for change.

I want you to find a way to **make a better life** for yourself, your family, and your community.

I want you to **feel the joy that comes from walking across that stage and holding that degree in your hand**. I want your families to experience that joy with you.

I want you to know that while college may not be the answer to all of your problems, there are **some doors that cannot be opened without a college degree**.

I want you to have whatever it takes to **help you find a job or career later in life that inspires you** to rise early, anxious to get to work because you find so much joy in doing it.

I want you to **feel the freedom** that comes from knowledge and wisdom.

I want you to **know what it takes to be a successful scholar** both in high school and in college.

I want you to see the scholarship process, especially the personal narrative essay that often accompanies that process, as **something that you can accomplish**.

I want you to remember to **press the pen down hard** as you write so as to leave an impression on things you were not intending to impress.

I want for **every one of your dreams to come true**.

THAT FIRST SENTENCE

This story starts with a yardman.

(No! My is a much more urgent choice of pronoun and first word, much more so than this.)

Let's try again.

My story starts with a yardman.

(It's good. It's honest, direct, and to the point. It has some interesting sound qualities with the repeating *s* sounds in *story* and *stop*. There is even a lovely poetic metrical cadence that happens near the end: *with a* YARD*man*. But is it too simple?)

Let's try again.

There will be no Odysseus, Hamlet, or Jay Gatsby in this story. This not a story of kings or fools. The main character of this story would suffer neither. This is the story of how one simple yardman inspired my path toward scholarship.

(This is also good, but is it too verbose? Does it go out of its way to insert material I definitely learned in high school with the literary allusions that open the passage? What if I use the technique of zooming in for a close-up, focusing on a place rather than a person and expanding outward from there?)

Let's try again.

The small wooden shelf in the sala had a gangster lean. Really the only thing holding it up was the weight of the word upon it.

(Will code-switching from living room to sala—which was the word I used as a child—be too challenging for the reader? I hope not. Surely, they can Google sala and find out what I mean with little inconvenience. Is the first sentence too conversational? Is the use of the word upon out of place in such proximity to a phrase like gangster lean? For me, and I hope for you, the answer is no. Every word in the English, Spanish, and Spanglish lexicons belong to me.)

This is how it begins. Or rather it begins this way for some of us—not with one possible thesis sentence, but with a handful. You might choose the best of the bunch, or you might take parts from each, creating a Frankenstein thesis sentence made up of the most effective parts of a few different starting points. You should ache over your first sentence because…it's your first sentence. This is where the reader gets their first glimpse of you, a glimpse that could be the difference between winning a scholarship or not. The first sentence is that important. Always remember that.

THIS IS A SCHOLARSHIP STORY, NOT A LOVE STORY

(But Then Again Maybe It's Both Happening At The Same Time)

My story starts with a yardman. For those of you who don't know what a yardman is, that's someone who parks their 1946 primer gray truck at the curb, walks to your front door and knocks confidently. Three times. Not enough to intimidate you but enough to let you know there is someone with purpose at your door. Then he wipes the sweat flowing down the furrows in his brow with a red bandana and swiftly folds it into a perfect square. People love perfect squares. When you answer the door, he will ask you in the best, broken English that he can if he can mow your front or back yard. Edge the grass. Rake and bag your leaves.

He will go on to tell you that you can pay him anything you think is fair. He will allow you to set his worth. He is that selfless. This man is mi Abuelo, my grandfather. My grandfather raised me when my mother could not and my father would not. So, to me, he was more than a simple yardman. He was my grandfather, and my mother, and my father, and my first teacher. Every word I've written in life, every scholarship or writing award I have ever received is because of this man.

To know him, you need to know what his workday looked like. My grandfather worked when the sun was up. I'm from Texas y'all. (I'm a Brown man but I can say y'all; I was born in Texas.) Texas is a desert, which means the sun is up all the time. So my grandfather's workdays were 12, 13, 14 hours long.

We lived in a little house he rented for us. A tiny dilapidated two-bedroom house with one bathroom, which belonged to all of us, and a kitchen that belonged only to my Abuelita Juanita, my grandmother. Our home was in a neighborhood called Barrio Eastside. We lived in the shadows of downtown Dallas.

There wasn't much work to be found in the city. So my grandfather would rise before the sun and journey to far off foreign suburbs. Places like Plano, Texas, and Garland, Texas. Places I didn't even know existed as a mocoso, a snotty-nosed kid from the barrio. In fact, the only thing I knew about planet Earth was the barrio of the lower east side that was my home. I thought the only place on the entire planet you could buy food for your family was a little grocery store called Yerry's Super Mercado, which some people called Jerry's Super Market for some reason. I thought the only place you could get a haircut was Roy Hernandez's Barbershop over on Henderson Ave.

But there was a much larger and scarier world out there beyond the sanctuary of my barrio, and my grandfather braved those treacherous lands six days a week. My grandfather worked Monday through Saturday. He believed Sunday belonged to Someone else. Wanting to make sure he had as many working hours as possible out in the suburbs with their sprawling yards, he would rise long before I did for school and come back home long after the sun would set.

He was mystified by the people who lived out there. It was the things that they did, that we would never dream of doing that perplexed him most. They would take things they no longer wanted and simply put them out on the curb for anyone to have. Bicycles with flat tires and rusty chains? Forget about it...a tube patch kit, some air, a little WD40, and that rusty Schwinn was as good as new. "Go on mi'jo, ride like the wind," he would say, and I would ride like the wind on my second hand bike.

TVs with broken antennas. Okay scholars let me explain. Back in the day, (that's how you know someone's old—when they use the phrase, *back in the day*) televisions used to have these two antennas—rabbit ears they were called—mounted on top of the television, and if they were perfectly straight you and your family could get all five of the channels. All *five* of them. (Be grateful you live in the time that you do.) But when one of those antennas would bend to the point of breaking, someone in that family would get so enraged they would take the whole TV antenna and all out to the curb for anyone to have. My grandfather would snatch it up and bring it back to our home. With the help of a little duct tape, aluminum foil, and someone holding the antenna that never seemed to hold its position for some godforsaken reason at just the right angle (me) we would get channel 4.

"Stop mi'jo freeze, don't move! We got the Cowboy game."

"But it's black and white Abuelo, which one are we?"

"The team with the star on the helmet mi'jo." This was my youth.

Back then they had recycling bins in those distant suburban neighborhoods. There are some neighborhoods today in my city that don't have recycling bins. But when those recycling bins all those years ago would fill up with newspapers, magazines, and the like, some of the people living in those suburbs would place entire boxes of books beside the recycling bin. This was my grandfather's most sought after treasure. When it came to books, he never used the word, *basura*, or trash. He always used the word *tesoro*, or treasure. He was a treasure hunter as well.

He would bring the books home and stack them on a little two-tier shelf in the sala (living room). That shelf they rested on had a gangsta' lean. Why did that little shelf lean precariously to the left? Because my grandfather found it on the side of the road! Really the only thing holding the shelf upright was the weight of the word upon it.

You already know I'm Latinx. You know how my people are. We reproduce. In great number. Activist and civic leader Dr. Juan Andrade Jr. often says, not only will we overcome, but with the current reproduction rate of Latinos, we will overwhelm.

With that being said I come from a large familia (family). We were spread out all over the city, but I lived in a casita (little house) in Barrio Eastside of Dallas. My grandfather was often fond of saying, "Cada vez que alguien en la familia pasa por momentos difíciles, pueden venir a quedarse con nosotros hasta que se mejoren las cosas." Whenever anyone in the family falls on hard times they can come and stay with us until they get back on their feet again.

My family lost their footing and their way more times than I can recall, so the home of my youth was constantly full of loud, passionate people. Although there was always a large number of people living in my grandfather's little house at any given moment of my youth, only one person in that entire familia had to read every one of those books on that little wooden shelf. That one person...was me.

My grandfather made me read them aloud to him late at night when he would return home from work. Mowing front and back yards in ever decreasing squares gave my Abuelo a love of patterns. The pattern for his day was as follows:

1. *Rise before the sun and head out for work.*

2. *Work all day under the unforgiving Texas sun.*

3. *Return home long after the sun had gone down.*

4. *Have his shower.*

5. *Hug my Abuelita Juanita during those years my grandmother was still with us.*

6. *Have his comida.*

7. *Retire into the sala where I had to read aloud to him for the better part of an hour.*

He did this six days a week. The only day my grandfather would not work was Sunday. He believed that day belonged to Someone else.

Picture in your mind a mocoso (snotty-nosed kid) with a curse word for the world holding a book of poems by William Blake reading them aloud to his grandfather in the evenings of his youth...when all he wants to do is run the streets with the other wild boys from the barrio. This was my youth. But one evening while reading a poem to my Abuelo, it happened. My grandfather who was a large, stoic man was moved to tears by a poem that I was reading aloud to him. Moments later in the middle of another poem a smile formed that spread from one side of his face to the other. The

16

strongest man I would ever know could be moved to tears or laughter by words. There was power in words. A power I yearned for.

And that's when I knew whatever I did for a living as an adult, I wanted it to involve words. I decided as a very young person that at some point in my life I wanted to be paid to be around words all day. I knew there would only be one way to attain this goal—college.

I started thinking about college as early as middle school. Middle school was a challenging existence to say the least. I attended Spence Middle School in East Dallas, which besides being a public middle school in Dallas, was also a TAG Academy. TAG stood for Talented and Gifted. Being a poor, skinny, Brown kid from the barrio I considered myself neither talented nor gifted. Yet because of my grades in elementary school I was placed in the TAG program.

It's funny to think about those formative middle school days, how they started and ended. I would walk to school with all of the other mocosos from the barrio, laughing and cracking on each other all the way there. Then as we approached the front door and walked in, we would dab each other by bumping fists and all of them would turn left and enter the public school side of the middle school campus, while I would turn right into the TAG academy.

The challenges I faced were intimidating but thrilling, especially in English, creative writing, journalism, history, anything that involved a great deal of reading and writing. I kept finding myself leaning into the page, pressing the pen down hard when I wrote. I had yet to learn that I just might be leaving an impression on things I was not intending to impress. Under this desire to learn more about becoming a more effective writer was my dream of attending college.

I began researching colleges that had excellent English and creative writing departments in middle school. It was then that I discovered a campus that years later would not seem too far from home for me but seemed like a world away at the time. It was a college that had an incredible English department and an impressive creative writing department. It was located in a city that I had never seen but had always been told was beautiful. In fact, most of what I knew about that city I would learn from my tío (uncle) Junior on those holidays when he would visit us from the far away city he had moved to as a young man to take a good job at the airport there.

This university was going to be my haven. My sanctuary. This university was not only going to be my way out of the barrio but my way back into to it to create change for my people. This goal of giving back to my people and helping to create change for them was instilled in me by my Abuelo and my tío Silastino, who was the biggest, strongest and most intimidating of all of my uncles. The plan was set into action. I decided right there and then that I would attend no other school. I was taking my talents to Austin, Texas, and I was going to be a Longhorn. I was going to be attending The University of Texas at Austin for my undergrad degree.

Even though I took honors or Advanced Placement math courses in high school, it was never a passion of mine, but it was time to begin thinking about the math.

In 1990, when I planned to attend the University of Texas as an incoming first year college student, I needed to find out the numbers associated with attending the largest university in Texas. When I found them, it was staggering. This is what it looked like:

$7500 - Tuition per semester for accepted in state students

$800 - Books and supplies

$8000 - Room and board

$7500 + $800 + $8000 = $16,300 per semester

$16,300 X 8 semesters (for my undergrad degree) = $130,400

At that exact moment in my life, I had one dollar and 25 cents of the sparest change in my pocket, which left me exactly $130,398.75 short of my goal of going to college.

I knew that my family was what the rest of the world considered poor. And yes, in terms of socioeconomic structures, we were that. But we were wealthy in love, faith, tacos, and all the things that really mattered. With that being said I knew as early as middle school that my Abuelo was making just enough money as a yardman who also occasionally picked cotton to just make ends meet. I knew that after rent, bills, food, and what he gave to the church, there was nothing left for us or me. I don't fault him for that. In fact, I was always so proud of just how hard he worked to ensure we had a roof over our heads and tortillas and frijoles in our bellies. My grandfather, my grandmother, and my tíos were there for me in so many ways as a child. But when it came to paying for my college education, I knew my family would not be able to help me. Something else would have to be done.

I first heard the word "scholarship" in middle school. As part of a talented and gifted program the teachers did a steadfast job of informing us about the joys and rigors of college at an early age. When I found out that scholarship meant free money...money that I or my family never had to pay back...ever, I was in.

A thought occurred to me when I found out about athletic scholarships—soccer! I had been playing for a handful of years already. Then a sobering memory quickly set in. When I was so very young I asked my tío Silastino, (the biggest and strongest and most tattooed of all of my uncles) to enroll me in soccer. I remember telling him, "Tío, I think someday I could be a professional soccer player. Someday, I think I could help the US win the World Cup!" He simply drank his morning coffee, unimpressed by my newfound passion. He was the only one of my uncles or aunts to never marry, and I was the only child in the entire family who was fatherless, so he always looked out for me and believed in me. He said he would not only sign me up, but he himself would take me to practices and all of the games.

My first season of soccer was coming to an end and things were not going as well as I had hoped. This reality hit me in the face like a wayward soccer ball had earlier in the week in practice when Chris Cantu had rung my bell on a free kick with a blast that struck me square on the nose.

It was our last game. We struggled. That last game was a microcosm of our entire season. After the game, most parents were consoling their children with promises of a trip to Braum's Ice Cream to soothe tiny bruised knees and egos. However, my tío Silastino, ever the realist, got down on one knee and looked me directly in the eye, so as to not look down on me as he was talking to me, the way most adults do when they have something to say to children. He was so good about that kind of thing. Even though I was only six years old, I'll never forget that conversation.

"Mi'jo." (My son or my little one.)

"Si tío."

I remember at this point he placed his hand gently on my shoulder. "You still want to be a professional soccer player when you grow up?" Questions asked in declarative statements, a trait common among all of my uncles.

"Si tío."

"Mi'jo...quiero decir esto con el debido respeto y afecto, pero..."

One thing you should know about my tío Silastino is that whenever he said, *I mean this with all due respect and affection but...*, he was about to curse you out in Spanish.

He continued, "I mean this with all due respect and affection, but...you suck. Like a lot. Like you scored two goals today...on your own team! The whole game you were running that way when we were all yelling for you to run this way. But look you're just a kid. Your destiny has yet to be laid out for you. Who knows where it will take you, how you will get there. Look at those little books you read. We've been checking out those books for you from the library for a couple years now already. They're small books for children, but they're books nonetheless. Hell mi'jo, you've read more books in the last year than I have in my whole lifetime. Your teachers are constantly telling us what a great student you are. The running joke in our family is you said your first thousand words before you took your first thousand steps. Maybe it's words mi'jo. Maybe words will be a way out of the barrio for you. Maybe words will be a way back in to save us all." He tousled my hair and we walked together to his truck. I have never forgotten that conversation with my uncle.

I continued to play soccer throughout the years. I got better. Even good...but not good enough to earn an athletic scholarship. I knew this. So, I decided as early as middle school that if I was going to earn a scholarship to college, I would have to use my mind to earn it, not my feet. With that being said, I worked HARD in middle school. As I was beginning to plan for my transition into high school, I knew I was going to be on a Pre-AP/AP track, which would require me to work even HARDER in high school to do what it takes to earn an academic scholarship. It was the summer between my last year in middle school and my first year in high school. I knew that life was going to be different for me in the fall. But I had no idea that my life would change forever in one violent moment that summer.

I can divide my life into two parts. The Light when my Abuelo was with me. And the Dark when he was not. Late one night, during the summer that followed middle school, my grandfather was driving back home to us from work in some far-off foreign suburb. He had reached the city, when some drunk fool ran a red light and crashed into my grandfather's 1946 Dodge truck. My grandfather was wearing his seat belt, but both cars and trucks made during that time only had the belt that went around one's waist, not the modern kind that go both over the shoulder and waist. When the impact happened my grandfather's body jerked forward with such force that his head struck the steering wheel and he broke his neck instantly.

The doctors told us at the hospital that my Abuelo would live for eight hours. My grandfather lived for eight days.

My mother had me when she was seventeen years old, but she was younger, more beautiful, and more rebellious than most seventeen-year-olds can be at that age. So, she was out in the barrio of my youth busy being young and beautiful and rebellious.

My father left my mother the year I was born and never returned. That's the beginning, the middle, and the end of the story of my father.

With that being said, my Abuelo raised me when my mother could not and my father would not. After his death, the family scattered to neighboring suburbs that may have been on the other side of the world to a skinny, Brown kid from the barrio of the inner city. In one tragic and foolish moment I lost my entire family. I lost my support system. I lost everything...or rather it was taken from me.

During high school I bounced around from couch to couch, from friend's house to friend's house, from family member to family member, but I never lasted more than a few months at any given place. I was an angry, young man with a curse word for the world. A world that allowed my grandfather's death to happen so needlessly. When I didn't have a couch to crash on, I would sometimes stay at the Austin Street Center for the homeless. When I would arrive there too late be able to get one of their cots, I would sleep on a bench that was enclosed in a tunnel near Lee Park. This was my high school experience—all while trying to be an astonishing student who could somehow earn a scholarship to the University of Texas at Austin.

I actually enrolled myself in high school and I had to have an address on file so I used the address of my tío's Silastino's apartment, which was in the district that allowed me to attend Woodrow Wilson High School in East Dallas.

My senior year arrived and not a moment too soon. I was 18 and impossibly exhausted and bewildered by life. I had worked with such diligence and dedication as a student. A student without a home to call his own. Late in the spring semester of my senior year my uncle called me and asked me to come pick up a letter that was mailed to him but addressed to me.

The letter was from the University of Texas at Austin and it read,

Dear Joaquín

We at the University of Texas at Austin would be honored to offer you a full ride, academic scholarship covering tuition, books, room, and board...

For those of you unfamiliar with the terms room and board, that meant my dorm room and meal plan were going to be covered. Not only was I going to college for free, I was going to have access to three meals a day. As someone who went to bed hungry many nights as a young person this meant the world to me. I was also going to have a room and a bed to call my own for the first time in a very long time. My dream had come true!

But let's rewind the story one year. Now I'm a junior in high school. My junior year of high school, I met...a girl. Every great story has one, even a scholarship story. She was wearing a red, backless dress as she walked into the West End Marketplace where we both worked during high school. I remember turning at the exact moment that I saw Aída for the first time to my friend Eric Thompson who worked with me at Amy's Ice Cream, and I said to him, "There goes the future mother of my children." He laughed and called me a romantic fool under his breath as he sampled the Belgium chocolate. Little did he know that she would actually be the future mother of my children.

It took weeks for me to work up the courage to ask her out. She was, after all, everything I was not. She was smart; I was not. She was beautiful; I was not. She was cool; I was a merd. You know what a merd is don't you? Mexican nerd.

Then one day I asked her out on a date, and she said...yes. Then we went on another date...and another, and another. Within months, we decided not date anyone else, but...us. Before I knew it a year had gone by, and I was beginning to think that I was falling...in...no. I refused to say that word. It was too big. I had loved someone completely with every fiber of my being, and after my grandfather's death, I had discovered what life was like after love. It was so damn difficult. I couldn't possibly fall in love. I was, after all, heading to my dream school in the fall.

So I decided that after a year of falling in whatever word I could displace for love, I had to break up with the most astonishing woman I would likely ever meet. I had to break up with her. It would not be long before I left for Austin and devoted every second of my life to my undergrad degree. We had a date scheduled for Friday night, and I decided that would be the moment.

We agreed to meet on the third floor at the West End Marketplace Laser Tag Center. This was no ordinary laser tag center. There were smoke machines and a laser show involved. We suited up, smiled as they handed us our laser guns, and decided at the last minute to battle on different teams.

In a matter of moments, we were separated from one another. I had lost sight of Aída in the simulated fog, and found myself wandering aimlessly in a large tunnel. All of a sudden, I felt a dull thud as I bumped into someone directly behind me. I spun around with my gun drawn. It was her. She had her gun drawn as well. This was the moment. The letter from UT was in my back pocket. I was about to reach for it. Instead I chose to lower my gun, lean in, and I sofity kissed her on the lips.

Then she shot me dead. Just another one of the myriad of reasons I had fallen in love with her.

I was reaching for the letter when she asked me, "Joaquín, can I tell you something I've never told anyone else in my entire life?"

"You're the best person I know. You're my best friend. My best everything. You can tell me anything." What she told me was…unspeakable. I cannot tell you what she told me because it is her truth to tell. But she has given me permission to tell you the edge of the story, the shallow before the depth of it.

What she told me had to do with her biological father who she was living with, and the word, *abuse,* and then the words, *10 years.* And now I knew in my fingertips, my bones, and my heart that I had two choices. I could find an adult who could offer her a few services to find a safe place for her and get her out of the hell she was living in…or I could be that person for her. I could go to my uncle's house that night and borrow some money from him for a deposit on a small apartment. I could go to another of my tío's houses and borrow some money from him for the ring I saw the other day in that pawnshop. I could go that night and take both her and her possessions from the house where this monster disguised as a father lived. I could never tell her about the scholarship. And I could trade my scholarship for the chance to see what love could teach me about life.

That's what I did. And we have been married a *long* time.

My young wife and I had a plan. A plan that began with college, followed by grad school, which would preface backpacking through Europe to find ourselves, followed by careers, then lastly followed by children.

Life, however, as you may already know has a way of interrupting the most well laid out plans.

A few months after we got married, we found out Aída was pregnant and that Aiyana our first daughter would be joining our family a full decade ahead of schedule. To this day, we never use the word *accident*; she was, is, and will always be our *surprise* baby. That's the perfect word for it.

We went to college the unconventional way. First, we had to put aside any thoughts of our dream colleges and look at more affordable universities to pursue. We ended up 30 minutes north of our hometown of Dallas in Denton, Texas, where my wife attended Texas Women's University, and I attended the University of North Texas. It wasn't my dream school, but they had a solid creative writing department and an even stronger English department. At this point there would be no scholarship to help me in my endeavors and while we qualified for partial financial aid, the bulk of the cost of our college educations was going to be our own responsibility.

We knew at some point we were going to have to take out student loans, and we did. They took us well over a decade to pay off. Whoever wrote that there are no crueler words in existence than "student loans" was, without question, a nonfiction writer. Yet, even with student loans there was still the expense of books, rent, food, utilities, and diapers that financial aid and student loans failed to cover. So we had to seek out part time jobs.

I took the responsibility of finding a part-time job that would not only provide enough income to help my young family immensely but also allow me the time to attend university all while providing insurance for my wife and soon-to-arrive daughter. Seeking out a part-time job that both paid well and provided health and dental insurance for my wife, daughter, and me was not easy. I searched and searched to no avail. Then a friend of mine said to me, "I think UPS is hiring in the area, you should look into it Joaquín." I did. Sure enough, they were hiring. However, the only hub that was hiring was in Mesquite, Texas, which was 30 minutes south and east of Dallas. Here comes the tragic turn in the story—they were only hiring for one shift.

I read once that the "graveyard shift" got its name because centuries ago, cups were forged out of lead which would poison those who drank from them too often. Poison them so that they would fall into a coma so deep, that would decrease their heart rate and breathing rate that most people would simply think the person had died. Tales spread of people waking from their coma submerged six feet under the earth and being buried alive. Gravediggers in an attempt to prevent this, would tie a string to the presumably dead person's wrist and run it through a pipe to the surface where the other end was tied to a bell.

Gravediggers would then stay up all through the night and listen for the bells.

If one would ring out, the gravediggers would dig frantically to rescue the person clawing and no doubt screaming in the coffin under all that fresh dirt. These people were literally "saved by the bell." Thus the expression that stays with us to this day. Those gravediggers assigned to keep watch for the bells through the late hours of deep night and early morning worked the first "graveyard shift."

My job at UPS, which was part of their graveyard shift that began at 10 PM and ended at 5 AM, was not nearly that dramatic or poetic. I was a sorter. Packages as small as an envelope and as large as a big screen television made their way down a series of interconnected conveyer belts until they found their way to a large metal slide that spanned some 30 feet. A few other co-workers and I would take the packages that slid down to us and place them in their corresponding metal cage that moved slowly but steadfastly behind us. The cages crawled their way down to the trucks where the loaders took the packages and envelopes out of them and placed them on their corresponding shelf in the truck.

The warehouse that I worked in did not have air conditioning or heat. Having no heat was not an issue. Although my people are tropical, we are good at layering up. Having no air conditioning was cause for concern. I live in north Texas, which is a desert. There are years when we have 8 months of summer, a couple of months each of spring and fall, and a few weeks of winter. Summer days in Texas can be unforgiving, reaching temperatures of over 100 degrees for weeks on end.

Keep in mind—my apartment near campus was half an hour north of Dallas, while the UPS hub I worked at was half an hour south of Dallas. Here's how my days were structured:

1. *Leave for work at 9 PM. Drive one hour to work*

2. *Work in an uncomfortably warm warehouse, lifting boxes as efficiently as I could all night.*

3. *Drive an hour home from work entirely exhausted at 5 AM.*

4. *Take a shower, make breakfast for my wife and child, and head off to college.*

5. *Take morning classes every morning five days a week.*

6. *Come home between noon and 1 PM and watch my daughter while my wife attended college taking only afternoon classes, while trying my best to study.*

7. *Take a nap when my wife returned home from classes. My nap. I would sleep two to three hours a day, from 5 PM to 8 PM. I would wake up eat, shower again to wake myself up and head off to work, to start all over again.*

After six months of working at UPS, I started driving Saturday air for them, so now I was doing this six days a week. My wife let me sleep on Sunday. The entire Sunday. I usually slept between 18-20 hours on Sunday as my body was trying to catch up from sleeping only a handful of hours during the week. I lost an entire day of the week for four years of my life. To this day my wife lets me sleep late any damn day I want because there was a four-year period of my life where I sacrificed sleep for both the good of my college education and the future of my family.

Earning my undergrad degree was simultaneously one of the most challenging and life-affirming accomplishments of my life. There wasn't anything easy about it, but my beautiful wife is so fond of the saying, "Nothing in life worth having comes easy." To this day I challenge my two daughters and all of my students to work so very hard in middle school and high school, so that they might place themselves in a position to attend college through the act of scholarship and enjoy the college experience. I can tell you that every teacher, counselor, librarian, assistant principal and principal that you have ever come in contact with does not want you to have to work as hard as I did during my undergrad college years. We want you to luxuriate in the experience of being a college scholar. It's understandable if you want to take a part-time job one to two days a week to earn a bit of extra money. Not only is that understandable, it's the kind of thing that builds character, but we don't want you working six days a week and sacrificing sleep and your health simply to make ends meet. We want you to simply be a college scholar. If this book seeks to accomplish anything, it is to help you put yourself in a situation where you can simply be and enjoy all that it is to be a college scholar without the added stressand fear of not knowing how your college experience will be paid for.

When I look back at photos and videos of my wife and I walking across that stage and being handed our degrees, our eyes are engulfed in tears. We cried partly for the fact that we had accomplished something that seemed impossible for so long. We cried partly for the fact that despite all the trials and tribulations, we never stopped believing in each other. We never stopped pushing the other when we needed a gentle (and often not-so-gentle shove). We never stopped finding time to laugh and reward ourselves for that A on an exam or essay. We never stopped loving each other.

I said this was not a love story. This was a scholarship story. Maybe I was wrong. And right. Maybe it was both, happening at the same time.

ROOM 219: LIFE AFTER COLLEGE

After receiving my degree, I turned in my eight weeks notice to the company I worked for four years, UPS. Now usually when someone quits a job they offer the company a two-week notice letting their boss know that they would be stepping down from their position to tackle a new endeavor. Sometimes out of gratitude and respect the employee offers more notice upwards of four to six weeks. I was so grateful to UPS for providing me with a job opportunity that allowed me to be a working, college student while offering my family not only health but dental insurance that I felt I owed it to them to offer them eight weeks notice.

As I turned in the letter stating that I would be stepping down in two months, the shift supervisor said to me, "Joaquín, may I ask what you are going to be doing?" "Oh, I'm taking a job as a teacher," I replied. My degree was a Bachelors of Arts and Sciences with a Major in English and a Minor in Secondary Education.

"May I ask what your starting salary is going to be as a teacher Joaquín?"

"No, I don't mind at all. My starting salary is going to be $23,700 a year." (This was years ago. Starting salaries have gone up significantly. If you are considering becoming a teacher, don't let the quoted figure steer you away from teaching. Again, this was years ago and believe me, the world is desperate for great teachers.)

"Joaquín, you have been driving Saturday next-day air for us for a few years and we are prepared to offer you a full-time position as a driver. We are prepared to offer you the East Dallas route you have been driving, which is the old neighborhood you grew up in. We are also prepared to offer you a starting salary of $48,000 a year, with an almost certain opportunity for overtime that would push you easily near $60,000 a year. Would you consider staying on?"

I simply said to them, "Thank you so much, for everything, but no. I'm so excited to be a teacher. I simply can't wait to start my life as a teacher. Plus, I just told my wife in two months that when I leave I will never lift another cardboard box in this lifetime. I am so grateful to you all for all you have done for me and my family, but I am out of here."

I count this as one of the best decisions I have made in this lifetime. I was a public high school English teacher for the best seven years of my life before writing my first collection of poems and stepping away from teaching. However, while I was on campus I arrived early every morning and stayed late every afternoon. I loved teaching. I couldn't wait to get to work and start my day. Not many people get to say that to themselves as they start their workday. I was nominated for teacher of the year seven years in a row. I won it twice. Much of what I present in this book I learned from those miraculous students who walked through the door simply labeled, *Mr. Z. Room 219.*

I came to that room to teach them. I hope that I did. What I didn't realize back then was just how much I would come to learn from them. This book is for Collette, Jon, Tim, Annika, Mason, Megan, Tomás, Marco, Tristan, Jessica, and all of the students I was honored to work with all those years in my classroom. Room 219. A room that was so small, yet so large. So simple, but so beautiful. I remember a conversation with a student in my classroom after school. She asked me, "How can I be a better student? How can I earn a scholarship to help my family pay for my college?" I hope this book answers these questions for her. And you.

FACING YOUR FEARS

(For Parents)

As our children begin the transition from high school to college scholars, it is only natural that trepidation sets in for us. However, we must be able to come to terms with and cope with that fear. After all, our children are counting on us to prepare them, and instill in them the courage it takes to face challenges that may take place while at college, possibly far from home.

My partner affectionately refers to one of our daughters as "Dropsy"; the other she lovingly calls "Tripsy." When we began to realize that one day these two young women would venture far away from us to attend college, we began taking steps to prepare them for the challenges that come with being an independent young woman at college. We created an open dialogue, having purposeful conversations about difficult topics.

Reading articles together written about young adults involved in car accidents because of texting while driving can be a challenging moment to have as a family, but it's a necessary one. The same is true for open discussions about the dangers of drinking and driving. College is going to be filled with parties that will likely involve alcohol. Creating an open and honest dialogue will not only better prepare them to face these kinds of situations with a level head, it will also go a long way toward putting your own mind at ease because you know you have done everything you can to prepare them to overcome the dangers of carelessness and recklessness.

Unfortunately, we live in a world where even our safest places like schools and churches can sometimes be filled with violence and danger. It's an ugly truth, but a truth nonetheless. Again, open dialogue and honest conversations about uncomfortable things like exit strategies and knowing how to seek out and find help and protection from authorities is necessary to ensure your child's safety when away from home. Reinforcing the fact that there is safety in numbers and challenging them to travel in groups at night can go a long way to making their college experience not only educational, but also a safe one. I hope to God that someday these conversations will no longer be needed, but unfortunately, they still are.

My wife enrolled herself and both our daughters in a self-defense class when they were teenagers. This may seem extreme, but my wife is a survivor of sexual assault, and she wanted to do everything in her power to make sure what happened to her never happened to one of our daughters. I attended those self-defense classes from time to time to watch their progress, and seeing the sense of pride in my daughters' eyes as they kicked or punched with great force made me feel as though we were doing right by them. These kinds of classes aren't for everyone, but if your child wants to try to learn self-defense and they seem to enjoy and grow from that experience, then perhaps the investment in time, energy, and money will be well worth it.

In short, keep doing the good work of parenting that you are already doing. Hopefully your children will not be overwhelmed in college when it comes to money, because you have gone over how to budget money with them on many occasions. They will know how to iron a shirt because you taught them that skill. What you have taught them about patience, kindness, selflessness, and strength will always stay with them. Know that.

In my journeys, I have occasionally come across Latinx students who tell me their parents are dead-set on them not going away to their dream college, but rather staying closer to home at a college not of their own choosing, but of their parents' choosing. I truly believe this stems from fear as well. We sometimes fear what will happen to the family business without that extra set of hands that our daughter or son offered. Perhaps deep inside of us, in places we don't like to think about, we fear being overcome with loneliness when our child leaves. I ask you as a parent myself not to think of what the family will be losing when your child has gone away to college, but rather all they will gain while they are there. Just imagine what they could accomplish with a college education. Instead of helping out the family by washing dishes in the kitchen, they could design a more energy-efficient kitchen. They could help develop a digital retail plan to help give the family business an online presence.

Lastly, I'm going to ask you as parents to do what I'm going to ask your children to do: simply trust the faculty and staff of their chosen university. I firmly believe that professors, academic advisors, and guidance counselors are extraordinary people. They want to serve your children, which is why they chose the professions that they did. Trust that they will do everything in their power to safeguard your children.

FACING YOUR FEARS

(For Scholars)

In a recent discussion with college bound high school seniors, I asked them to discuss some of their fears they had about going off to college in small groups. Let's briefly discuss each of these fears and what you as a student can do to combat them, and come to terms with the fact that you are extraordinary—that makes you larger than any fear you could ever face in life. Remember: every problem in life has a solution. Sometimes just remembering this simple premise goes a long way toward making you feel more confident in the face of fear.

1. Being assigned a roommate that you don't like

There is a possibility that you will be assigned a roommate who is rude, loud, or messy. However, I imagine you will be so busy during those first few weeks of college that you may not even have time to notice those traits of your roommate. Be patient and understanding, and do everything in your power to have open and honest conversations with your roommates about how you like to live and vice versa. If the roommate's unsettling behavior continues to bother you, you can always bring in an arbitrator like a Residence Hall Advisor to help you both grow into more compatible roommates.

2. Classes that are much more challenging than high school classes

It goes without saying that classes in college will be more challenging than classes in high school. However, some classes like Pre-AP and AP courses, will prepare you for the rigors of college courses. Just by reading this book, you're doing the good work of preparing yourself for the challenges that you will face your freshmen year of college. One of the best pieces of advice I can give you to succeed in challenging college courses is to utilize Office Hours that your professors offer. Meeting and working with a professor in a one-on-one setting can allow you time to ask questions that you did not get to ask in class. Consider joining or forming a study group for classes that are bewilderingly difficult as well.

3. Professors who are not nearly as kind and gentle as your high school teachers

Your professors are passionate human beings. They have mastered the work they profess, so it stands to reason that they would be well versed and incredibly passionate about the topic. However, under that well-tailored blazer is a human being. Trust that they are there to serve you. If you feel they are moving too fast and you're having difficulty keeping up, ask for permission to tape class, either in an audio or video format, so you can review it later that night. Again, take advantage of the Office Hours they offer to have them help you go over perplexing material.

4. Combating loneliness

One of the best ways to combat loneliness is to be involved with and become a part of your campus. Join student organizations. Take advantage of intramural clubs and extracurricular activities. Your roommate may want you to go to the football game with them. A member of your study group may want you to attend a student poetry slam on campus with them. A classmate may ask you to accompany them to a movie at the college movie theatre. You are there to study and learn, but you're also there to experience social activities, make relationships and have fun.

Don't be afraid to use FaceTime or Skype to call home. Believe me, your parents are desperate to talk to you and see your face. Sometimes all it takes is a smile from mom or a corny joke from dad to make you realize you're not alone in this.

5. What to do when feeling homesick

Keep the lines of communication open. You and your family will have to find the right balance. You'll probably want your independence, and your family wants you to have it as well. Being on your own helps you develop a sense of self, but sometimes even the most independent of us need to see a familiar face or hear a familiar voice—and that's okay. If you prefer to have a scheduled Skype session once or twice a week at a set time, feel free to do so. If you prefer calls to be more organic, that's fine too. Remember that holiday breaks and visits home are not too far off in the semester. Keeping all of these things in mind will help you realize that everyone at home believes in you, and only wants the best for you. At the end of the day, you may feel lonely sometimes, but you will never be alone.

6. What to do about money

If you have a part-time job, financial aid, or funding from a scholarship that is also meant to cover your food and general living expenses, know that it's okay to worry about money. However, know that thanks to technology it is an incredible time to be a student trying to live within their means. Simply open your app store on your smartphone and type in "budgeting" in the search bar. There is a wealth of apps designed to help you budget your money as a student. Test a few out, and find the one that works best for you.

7. How to manage all the responsibilities that comes with being a college student

I'll talk more in the book about organization, but it starts and ends with planning and preparation. Again, find an app that can help you organize your assignments and due dates. Use reminders on your smart phone to help stay ahead of schedule. As old school as it may seem, I truly believe in the hand-held student planner. Many come with daily as well as monthly calendar pages that help you see what is due in the coming days, weeks, and months. Keep in mind that these apps and planners cost money. You're a struggling college student who shouldn't worry about such costs. Call your tío or your aunt and ask them to buy you that app or that planner. That's one of your uncle's jobs: to buy you academic planners and apps that help you stay organized.

8. Having to cook and clean

When in doubt about cooking or cleaning, Google it. You can also use YouTube to find out how to do just about anything from sautéeing vegetables in EVOO (Google EVOO) to checking your car's oil. My daughters have a nickname for me: "over-explaining dad." Yes, you can always call your parents or a family member for help. They want to help.

9. Getting lost (on campus and in life)

Familiarize yourself with your college campus map. Your college's website usually will have an interactive campus map that you can easily use to find your way. Don't be afraid to simply ask someone for help. Other students and staff feel like original settlers when they get to offer someone directions. It's a good feeling. Who knows, in a few weeks or months, you may even find yourself in a situation where you get to direct someone to the Student Union.

If you find yourself feeling lost in the larger sense of the word, seek help. There are advisors and counselors on staff who are there to serve you. Don't be afraid to reach out to them. Your emotional well-being is impossibly important in making your way as a college student. I have had to seek therapy in life, and so has my partner. That doesn't make us broken. It makes us human. Remember, we all need someone to help us cope with life from time to time.

10. The freshman 10, which can sometimes tragically turn into the freshman 15

Gaining ten or 15 pounds our freshman year happens to some of us, but the good news is there are things you can do to combat it. If you are going to fall into the traps of stress eating while studying for an exam, have healthy low-calorie snacks at your disposal. Some students approach the college buffet in the cafeteria as a challenge to eat until they are full. Others take it as a challenge to eat until they are tired. I remember saying to my partner once when we were both college students, "It's like they're challenging me to eat until I die!" Be wise in the college buffet line, don't take more food than you can eat, and make healthy choices. Find your way over to the salad bar for lunch, dinner, or both.

Stay active. Exercise or walk a handful of times each week. Join intramural clubs or take extracurricular activities. It's not just a good way to stay in shape, it's also a good way to make friends. You will make time to sharpen your mind. That's what college is about, but you also need to take time to care for your body. You will need both your body and mind to succeed in life.

I'm going to ask you in this book to seriously think about your future, especially as it relates to your future as a college or university scholar. As with anything, whether it be soccer or sewing, there is a world of terminology and diction, or words, associated with that specific activity or skill that you should be well versed in if you are going to attempt to master it. The same is true for college.

What follows is a list of words that you may already be familiar with, but if for whatever reason you are not, I have defined them here for you. These are words that will begin to be a part of your life as you prepare for college and as you make your way through the undergrad and graduate programs. Don't be intimidated by the words *undergrad* and *graduate program*; I will define those for you in a moment.

ACADEMIC WORDS TO KNOW AND NOT BE INTIMIDATED BY

Academic year: The school year that starts with autumn classes and concludes with spring or summer classes. The academic year at most US colleges and universities begins sometime in August or perhaps September and runs through May.

Advisor: A school staff member, usually assigned by your college or university, whose job is to help you develop a degree plan and help in choosing your classes to make sure you are taking the right courses to graduate.

Advocate: Advocates that may be staff members or fellow students on campus who provide resources for student survivors of trauma.

Associate's degree: A type of degree awarded to students at a junior college or community college, usually after two years of classes. Often times this degree is extremely cost effective as it usually requires less monetary investment than a degree from a four-year institution. This kind of two-year investment of time and energy usually means a wealth of transfer classes that a student can transfer over to their four-year college. There may even be a four-year college or university than will accept all of the credit hours earned from your Associates degree.

Audit: To attend a class without receiving academic credit. Keep in mind while this may be an option in some college classes, you may run across a professor that does not allow this for whatever reason. Be sure to check with the college or professor before auditing any class.

Bachelor's degree: A degree awarded to undergraduates, usually after four years of college classes.

Commencement: Day of graduation.

Course Number: The number your college or university assigns to a course. This number is usually needed in order to register for a class and can be found in the college catalog that list all classes available for that academic semester along with a course description and the accompanying course number.

Credit Hour: The number of hours assigned to a specific class. Credit hours vary per class, but usually range between one and five credit hours. Knowing that I would need five credit hours of math for my undergraduate or Bachelor's degree in English, I was able to find a five-hour pre-calculus class. While taking a single five-hour class in a fall academic semester was a challenge it was so extraordinary to end that semester and know that I would not have to take another math class in my life. The credit hour is usually the number of hours per week you are in the class. Let's say you have a three-hour English composition class—you might have to attend that class on Tuesdays and Thursdays from 10:00 AM to 11:30 AM, or an hour and a half two days a week, which adds up to a three-hour course. The number of credit hours you enroll in determines whether you are a full-time student or a part-time student. While each university or college may have their own way of determining what constitutes a full-time or part-time student, 15 hours is generally the norm for a full-time student. Anything above 15 hours is often referred to as a heavy load. I took 18 hours in one semester while working a part-time job, and it was quite demanding. There is an old saying that if the course is a three-hour course, you will need to set aside that many hours a week to study for it, but you will find that many three-hour courses require more study time than that. Still, other three-hour courses that you are naturally gifted in may come easier to you and require a little less study time. This is where your time management skills will pay off ensuring that you meet all the demands of your course load.

Doctorate: The highest academic degree, awarded after a bachelor's degree. Keep in mind, when most people think of a doctorate they think of a medical degree. A doctorate degree can be earned in many fields, such as education or physics. I myself am considering entering a doctorate program that would earn me a Doctorate of Philosophy with a concentration in poetry.

Elective: A class you can take that is not specifically required by your major or minor. Consider taking an elective that you will find enjoyable. Electives can be a great way to relieve the stress associated with the rigors of advanced course work. I took racquetball as an elective during my sophomore year and not only was it a great way to stay in shape, it was also a great way to take my mind away from the intense English classes that required a great deal of writing and reading I was often bombarded with as an English major.

Extracurricular activities: Groups you belong to outside of class, such as sporting teams, clubs and organizations. These can range in activities from soccer or flag football to disc golf or bowling. Extracurricular activities are a great way to make friends and develop a sense of belonging on your campus.

Financial Aid: Money you receive for your college tuition or expenses that you may or may not have to pay back. (See: "Grant," "Loan," and "Scholarship")

Freshman: Similar to the classifications you've experienced in high school, a freshman, or freshmore on some campuses, is a first-year college student.

Full-time student: A student who enrolls in at least a minimum number (determined by your college or university) of credit hours of courses. Again, this number varies at different universities or colleges but is usually in the neighborhood between 12 to 15 credit hours.

General education classes: Classes that give students basic knowledge on a variety of topics. In order to graduate students must sometimes (but not always) take general education classes. This set of classes includes different courses and can be called by different names at various colleges and universities.

Grade point average: The average of all of the course grades you have received, usually on a four-point scale. You may come across a program that does not use a grade point average system but rather has their own way of marking a student's progress and achievement, such as simply using a pass/fail project-based program.

Grant: A form of financial aid from a non-profit organization (such as the government) that you do not have to repay. Like the scholarship, this is the kind of financial aid I want you thinking about early and often.

Greek: Fraternities and sororities often identified by Greek letters. While being a member of a fraternity or sorority does require a student to often commit time to the organization, some students feel the support and camaraderie they offer as well as the offer of specific student housing options make that investment of time the right choice for them.

Internship: A temporary job, paid or unpaid, usually in the field of your major. You may be able to receive college credit for an internship.

Junior: Third-year college student.

Loan: (or Student Loan) A form of financial aid that you must repay. Often times that loan must be paid back with interest, and that interest grows over time, so you are actually paying back more than you borrowed. Remember a grant, scholarship, or certain other forms of financial aid you do not have to pay back; if at all possible, avoid student loans.

Major: Your primary area of study. Your college major is the field you plan to get a job in after you graduate (for example: business, linguistics, anthropology, psychology).

Master's degree: A degree awarded to graduate students. The awarding of a master's degree requires at least one year of study (often more, depending on the field) after a student earns a bachelor's degree.

Maymester: A short full academic semester compressed into one, two, or sometimes three weeks that is a precursor to summer sessions. These classes are not for the faint of heart or the scholar that has a problem with procrastination. Many times, the classes last several hours a day for the full three weeks, and will require an immense amount of out of class reading, writing, and studying. While it's a good way to get ahead of your degree program and perhaps graduate early, it is a daunting and taxing workload. I never took a Maymester class, but my partner did, and she said that it was the most challenging thing she ever did during her first undergrad degree without question. I remember there was a great deal of crying on her part at the end of that three weeks, partly due to the lack of sleep and stress she endured and partly due to the fact that it was behind her.

Minor: Your secondary area of study. Fewer classes are required for a college minor than for a major. Colleges and universities usually don't require students to have a minor. Many students' minors are a specialization of their major field. For example, students who want to become a science reporter might major in journalism and minor in biology.

Non-resident: A student who isn't an official resident of the state where a public university is located. Tuition at public universities is more expensive for non-residents.

Office hours: A specific time set aside by professors or teaching assistants for students to visit their office and ask questions or discuss the course they teach. Your professor or teaching assistant will tell you at the beginning of the term when and where office hours will be every week.

Online classes: Courses you take by computer instead of in a traditional classroom.

Part-time student: A student who doesn't enroll in enough credit hours to become a full-time student, as defined by your college or university. Part-time students often take only one or two classes at one time.

Prerequisite: A class that must be taken before you can take a different class. (For example, Astronomy 100 may be a prerequisite for Astronomy 200.)

Private university: A university that is privately funded. Tuition for a private college or university (before scholarships and grants) is the same for all students.

Public university: A university that is funded by the government. Public colleges and universities are less expensive for residents of the state where they are located.

Quarter: A type of academic term. A school following this system will generally have a fall quarter, winter quarter and spring quarter (each about 10 weeks long), along with a summer term. (See also: "Semester")

Resident: A student who lives in and meets the residency requirements for the state where a public university is located. Tuition at public universities is often less expensive for residents.

Scholarship: A form of financial aid that you do not have to repay. A scholarship is basically free money awarded to you that you must apply for, often requiring letters of recommendation, a high school or college transcript, an application packet, and an accompanying scholarship application essay.

Semester: A type of academic term. A school with this system will generally have a fall semester and a spring semester (each about 15 weeks long), along with a summer term that may actually be broken into two or three summer sessions. (See also: "Quarter")

Senior: Fourth-year college student. You are a senior when you graduate from college.

Sophomore: Second-year college student.

Syllabus: A description of a course which also lists the dates of major exams, assignments and projects.

Term: The length of time that you take a college class. (See also: "Quarter" and "Semester")

Transcript: An official academic record from a specific school. It lists the courses you have completed, your grades, and information such as when you attended the school.

As complicated as some of the terminology associated with college or university life can be, there is also a world of abbreviations and acronyms that you must also begin familiarizing yourself with. I know the previous and upcoming lists can be intimidating, but take them in parts. Don't attempt to learn and master all of this in one sitting. Tackle a few words and abbreviations a day. If you start to feel overwhelmed, step back and take a break. Remember—a successful scholar knows when to lean into the book and press the fingers down firmly onto the keyboard, but they also know when to step away from the desk and take the occasional break. Below is a list of common abbreviations and acronyms associated with the process of applying for college, a scholarship, or financial aid during your years as a junior or senior in high school as well as many associated with college or university life. *(Do keep in mind that with both the list of vocabulary and the list of common acronyms, some universities use their own terminology and abbreviations. These are provided here to give you a general background of the kinds of diction and abbreviations you might encounter.)*

ACADEMIC ACRONYMS AND ABBREVIATIONS TO KNOW AND NOT BE INTIMIDATED BY

ACT: Originally this acronym stood for American College Testing, but now the letters themselves hold no individual meaning. It is simply a three-letter term that means a national admissions examination, which functions in much the same way as the SAT to offer universities data, numbers, and writing samples to compare students from different schools.

ADCOM: Admissions committee.

BME: Biomedical engineering.

CAS: College of Arts and Sciences.

CC: Community College.

DE: Dual enrollment.

ECs: Extra Curriculars.

FA: Financial aid.

FAFSA: Free Application for Federal Student Aid.

FAO: Financial aid office or Financial aid officer.

GC: Guidance counselor.

HBCU: Historically Black Colleges and Universities.

IB: International Baccalaureate, an international educational foundation headquartered in Geneva, Switzerland, that offers educational diplomas or certificates for completion of one of their educational programs designed by their team of international teachers.

LAC: Liberal Arts College.

NCAA: National Collegiate Athletic Association.

NHS: National Honor Society.

OH: Office hours.

PG: Postgraduate year.

R+B: Room and board. Room refers to dorm room, while board refers to food or a meal plan.

RA: Rolling admissions.

RA: Resident Assistant. This is usually an upper class undergrad student or postgraduate student who lives in a resident hall or dorm building on campus, and is assigned the duty of making sure all hall rules are being adhered to.

SAT: A national college admissions examination.

STEM: Science, Technology, Engineering, Mathematics.

STEAM: Science, Technology, Engineering, Arts, Mathematics.

TCE: Total college experience.

UAA: University Athletic Association.

URM: Underrepresented minority.

WL: Wait list.

A LITTLE ELABORATION ON FAFSA

All of the above acronyms are important, but one is the most crucial: FAFSA. The Free Application for Federal Student Aid is absolutely essential if you want federal aid to help you attend college. Here are some of the things I want you to know about FAFSA:

1. *Everyone should file for it. It is free to file for FAFSA.*

2. *Fill it out early and remember it must be re-filed every year.*

3. *The fastest way to fill out the form is online at fafsa.gov.*

4. *If you're a dependent student, you will be using both your and your parents' information.*

5. *You're considered a dependent student if you are under 24 years old by December 31st of the school year you are applying, attending an associate's or bachelor's degree program, or are unmarried with no children or dependents of our own.*

6. *You will need the following documents ready to complete the FAFSA form: your social security number, tax information, records of income, records of your checking and saving account balances, driver's license number, and a list of schools you're interested in attending.*

7. *The FAFSA form can be intimidating, so go to your GEAR UP staff member, your guidance counselor, a favorite teacher, or your parent for help. Every adult in your school building wants to see you succeed and will do everything in their power to help you through the process, or get you to someone who can.*

Along the same lines of common abbreviations for the college and university experience lays the end result—the actual degree you are working to earn. These degrees traditionally take two, four, six, or eight years to earn, but can take longer for part-time students. On the other hand, students taking summer courses and heavy loads throughout any academic year can earn the following degrees in less than the traditional length of time. Also remember students taking dual credit courses in high school or those who do exceptionally well on the AP exam can actually begin day one of college with many college credits already under their belt. My daughter who took advantage both dual credit courses and the AP exams will be graduating this fall at age 20 with her Bachelor's in Forensic Science degree. That pace worked for her, but it might not work for you. You will know as you begin to work through the course load whether you will follow a traditional length of time in earning your degree, or a pace that is somewhat quicker or slower.

Associate's – traditionally two years to accomplish

Bachelor's – traditionally four years to accomplish

Masters – traditionally two to three additional years on top of the four years you dedicate toward earning your Bachelors

Doctorate – traditionally four additional years on top of the four years you dedicate toward earning your Bachelors

While there are countless degrees one can earn with a corresponding acronym—or short hand way of stating that degree—the degrees that follow comprise a partial list of common educational degree abbreviations. For instance, I hold a B.A. from UNT, or a Bachelor of Arts with a concentration in English from the University of North Texas. I also hold an MFA from IAIA, or a Master of Fine Arts with a concentration in Poetry from the Institute of American Indian Arts in Santa Fe, New Mexico. I have my sights set on a Ph.D. from UNT. One of the goals I have set for myself is to earn a Doctor of Philosophy with a concentration in Poetry from the University of North Texas in Denton, Texas.

COMMON EDUCATION DEGREE ABBREVIATIONS

A.A. – Associate of Arts

A.A.S. – Associate of Applied Science

A.S. – Associate of Science

B.A. – Bachelor of Arts

B.B.A. – Bachelor of Business Administration

B.E. – Bachelor of Education or Bachelor of Engineering

B.F.A. – Bachelor of Fine Arts

B.L.A. – Bachelor of Liberal Arts

B.S. – Bachelor of Science

M.A. – Master of Arts

M.B.A. – Master of Business Administration

M. E. – Master of Engineering

M.Ed – Master of Education

M.L.I.S. – Master of Library & Information Studies

M.F.A. or MFA – Master of Fine Arts

M.Th. – Master of Theology

D.A. or Art.D. – Doctor of Arts

D.B.A. – Doctor of Business Administration

D.Ed. – Doctor of Education

D.L.S. – Doctor of Library Sciences

D.M.A. – Doctor of Musical Arts

D.Sc – Doctor of Science

LL.D. – Doctor of Laws

Ph.D. – Doctor of Philosophy

D.D.S. – Doctor of Dental Surgery

M.D. – Doctor of Medicine

Pharm.D. – Doctor of Pharmacy

THE MAGIC QUESTION: HOW DO I DO IT?

I have now been away from teaching longer than I was a teacher. A big part of my current job as a poet and writer is to travel the country and share poems with audiences and teach poetry or creative writing workshops. But as a youth engagement specialist, another part of my job is to take my expertise as a writer and teacher and teach students all over the country everything I know about the scholarship process, especially as it relates to the personal narrative essay, in a workshop setting. My former department chair, Mrs. Matteson said it best to me. "You're still in front of students. You're still a teacher first and a poet second. For me, you were and always will be a teacher who moonlights as a poet." I love that so much. So, I travel the country like a Johnny Applesonnet working with migrant students in the RGV (Rio Grande Valley), or CAMP students in Georgia, or GEAR UP students in New Mexico as well as countless other states and programs. Inevitably in my travels the same question emerges.

One of the most often asked questions I receive from students is, *"How do you do it?"* The answer to the question, "How do I go about earning an academic scholarship?" is perplexing, to say the least. So, I went to the source. I've been blessed to work with some astonishing college and university students all over the country, many of them who have earned academic scholarships to get them there. I also work with successful high school students all over the country who are well on their way to earning scholarships. Who better to learn from than them? So I asked them and documented their answers then condensed those answers into the following:

COMMIT TO THE ACT OF BEING AN EXCELLENT SCHOLAR BOTH IN CLASS AND WHEN AWAY FROM CLASS

BE A PART OF YOUR CAMPUS

BE INVOLVED IN YOUR COMMUNITY

WRITE AN EFFECTIVE AND AWARD-WINNING SCHOLARSHIP ESSAY TO ATTACH TO YOUR PACKET

That's it. Were you expecting more? I was. But in every conversation I've had with successful scholars, it all comes down to these four basic premises. Let's look at each one in greater detail.

JOURNALING TO REFLECT, REJOICE, AND GROW

What I need you all to understand is that yes, I am a teacher, but I'm also a writer, and I use writing, especially the act of journaling, to promote growth within myself. So, you must understand that I am going to occasionally ask you to be my co-author inside this book by journaling and writing your truth and your experiences inside this actual book.

I write to get free, and I know that some of you do as well, just as I know some of you look forward to writing about as much as you look forward to a visit to the dentist. But both journaling and root canals are very necessary endeavors. And yes, at times, both can be painful, but ultimately we grow pain-free from both acts.

Please understand that if I challenge you to write about a moment of struggle, I do so not to amplify a memory that may have been extremely challenging for you, but to give you the opportunity to reflect and grow not only from your successes but from your struggles as well. My astonishing Puerto Rican partner always tells me when I write on social media about an award or accomplishment of mine as a teacher or poet, "You can't just write about your victories. You have to write about your failures too."

She's absolutely right. I grow as a teacher or poet when I reflect on a submission that was rejected by a literary magazine, or a workshop that was not accepted by a conference. A successful writer much like a successful scholar, is always reflective. Remember, when we write about our victories and our losses we do so not to bask in the negativity or positivity we were feeling at the time, but to get to the root of why we were either successful or not in those living, breathing moments.

"My father had a very simple view of life: you don't get anything for nothing. Everything has to be earned, through work, persistence, and honesty."

—Grace Kelly

There is so much truth in this simple premise. Working hard as a scholar will not guarantee you a scholarship, but I don't think I've ever met a scholarship recipient who was not a hard worker. When it comes to hard work, we are not just speaking of the hard work that happens between the bells that frame the beginning and end of class. Hard work extends well beyond the classroom. Let's examine how an effective student embraces the concept of hard work both in and out of the classroom.

Before we delve deeper into this, I need you to know that it is okay to feel struggle, to feel frustration, and yes to even feel failure. None among us is perfect. Even that scholar you see sitting far off in the distance in the cafeteria at the table engulfed with popular kids. You know the one I'm talking about—the one that everyone gravitates to because she seems perfect in every way. Even her...she sometimes feels overwhelmed by school and life, and yes on occasion she even feels defeated—and that's okay. It's what we do to overcome these setbacks that makes all the difference in the world.

WRITE, REFLECT, REPEAT

Write about a time in your academic endeavors when you felt as though you were defeated. Maybe it was a science project, research paper, or a group assignment that you just did not do well on for whatever reason. After you write about the actual moment—the setting, the time, the class and people involved, dig deeper. Then write about why you think you struggled. You could also write about all the things you might have done differently that would have made you a more successful scholar in that moment.

WRITE, REJOICE, REPEAT

Write about a time in your academic endeavors when you felt as though you were victorious. Maybe it was a science project, research paper, or a group assignment that you just did an extraordinary job on for whatever reason. After you write about the actual moment—the setting, the time, the class, the teacher, and people involved, dig deeper. Then write about why you think you succeeded. You could also write about all the study habits, scholarly skills, and work ethic that may have led to your success as a scholar in that moment.

THE BEAUTIFUL AND MADDENING GRIND OF SCHOOLWORK: HOW TO COMMIT TO THE ACT OF BEING AN EXCELLENT SCHOLAR

To begin, let's look at some habits of successful students. I have traveled the country working with high school students in creative writing and scholarship essay writing workshops. I always try to take advantage of those times and ask a few students what advice they would give a younger student who wants to be successful, the kind of student scholarship boards go out of their way to single out and award money for college. While their answers vary, they always seem to fall back on the following seven guidelines:

1. *Read.*

2. *Manage your time wisely.*

3. *~~Work~~ Study smart, not hard.*

4. *Take care of yourself, both physically and emotionally.*

5. *Avoid the trap of multi-tasking and distractions by concentrating on one task at a time.*

6. *Think of each test as an opportunity for success not an opportunity for failure or anxiety.*

7. *When it comes to both short term and long term goals...keep it real.*

Here's the kicker—the same advice holds true for both successful high school scholars and undergraduate and graduate scholars in college who are also thriving. It would seem there are several commonalities that all successful scholars share. That's another goal I have for this book—that it not only makes you a more marketable scholar worthy of receiving multiple academic scholarship offers, but that it also makes you a stronger and more effective scholar capable of facing all of the academic challenges that come your way.

1. READ

I firmly believe we would have more successful scholars both in elementary, middle, and high school if we had more successful readers in elementary, middle, and high school. Students in the past have asked me, "How do I become a better reader?" I often reply, "If you want to get good at a particular thing, hang out with that thing. If your tío (uncle) says to you, "Mi'jo (little one) today you will lift weights with me in the garage for one hour." Then the next day he says the same thing and makes you lift weights with him for one hour in the garage. And then at the end of that week he says to you, "Mi'jo today we are going to add two and a half pounds to each side." At the end of that second week and start of the third your tío then decides to take off the two and half pounds on each side. You smile, but it's a brief and passing moment of relief as your tío then says that after removing the two and a half pounds on each side of the barbell he will replace them with an additional five pounds on each side.

Your uncle repeats this act of adding a little more weight at the end of each week, and you stick to this routine of hanging out with and working diligently with weight. Do you know what you will be at the end of a month or two of this experience? Stronger.

The same is true for words. If you want to get stronger with words, if you want to become a more effective reader and writer—skills that are necessary to be a successful scholar in any class—then simply hang out with words. The best way to hang out with words is to read them, to look at the diction, sentence variation, and figurative language involved in crafting a masterful collection of poems, books of essays, or novel.

What an extraordinary time to be a reader, especially when it comes to reading the work of writers who are writing today. Thanks to the world of social media, a young scholar can read a book by an author or poet, reach out to them through the world of Twitter, or Instagram, or Facebook and ask them a question. Those writers won't always answer a young scholar, but sometimes they will. When that happens, that young scholar often turns into a life-long reader, and more importantly, a life-long scholar.

I want to give you a list of resources. Books, that I believe are good places for young scholars to begin looking for writers that will change them, charge them to action, and make them more effective scholars. Remember these lists are mine, but feel free to tweak them and make them your own. In fact, I want to make the first of several sections of this book into a Call and Response format. I will call out (write) 10 books I believe you should read, then you will respond with your list of 10 essential similar books you believe to be an absolute must read. If you cannot come up with 10 create a dialogue with teachers and friends to find 10 that they/you believe in.

CALL: 10 YA Novels Every Young Scholar Should Read

1. *The Hunger Games by Suzanne Collins*

2. *We Were Liars by E. Lockhart*

3. *The Hate U Give by Angie Thomas*

4. *Divergent by Veronica Roth*

5. *The Book Thief by Markus Zusak*

6. *Speak by Laurie Halse Anderson*

7. *The Fault in Our Stars by John Green*

8. *Ender's Game by Orson Scott Card*

9. *The Perks of Being a Wallflower by Stephen Chbosky*

10. *Bless Me, Ultima by Rudolfo Anaya*

RESPONSE: 10 YA Novels You Feel Every Young Scholar Should Read

1. _____

2. _____

3. _____

4. _____

5. _____

6. _____

7. _____

8. _____

9. _____

10. _____

*HW — Take a photo of your response and post it on social media with the hashtag #dollarsforscholars so other scholars can be inspired and challenged by your list, and you can be inspired and challenged to read the books on their lists.

CALL: 10 Books of Poetry Every Young Scholar Should Read

1. *Beastgirl & Other Origin Myths by Elizabeth Acevedo*

2. *Milk and Honey by Rupi Kaur*

3. *Citizen: An American Lyric by Claudia Rankine*

4. *Don't Call Us Dead by Danez Smith*

5. *The Princess Saves Herself in This One by Amanda Lovelace*

6. *Corazón by Yesika Salgado*

7. *The Rose that Grew from Concrete by Tupac Shakur*

8. *Red Suitcase by Naomi Shihab Nye*

9. *When My Brother Was an Aztec by Natalie Diaz*

10. *Crown by Natasha Carrizosa*

RESPONSE: 10 Books of Poetry You Feel Every Young Scholar Should Read

1. _____
2. _____
3. _____
4. _____
5. _____
6. _____
7. _____
8. _____
9. _____
10. _____

*HW — Take a photo of your response and post it on social media with the hashtag #dollarsforscholars so other scholars can be inspired and challenged by your list, and you can be inspired and challenged to read the books on their lists.

2. TIME MANAGEMENT

If you haven't already figured it out as a high school scholar, believe me you *will* figure it out as a college scholar, there are only so many hours in a day, week, and an academic semester. To be an effective student, you must start at the beginning. Knowing the time you have to commit to school, perhaps a part time job, and social engagements is crucial.

When was the last time you sat down at your desk or on your bed on a Sunday and looked at your week ahead? The assignments that are due each day. The group project meetings. The test in Calculus or the quiz in Spanish 3 you might have coming up that you know you need to set aside some time for. Keeping track of all of these commitments while thinking about your commitments to your family and friends can be a daunting task. However, pre-planning helps a scholar see the week or grading period ahead of them, and the scholar can prioritize tasks while keeping in mind the incessant ticking of the clock that refuses to slow down, let alone stop.

Make time on Sunday to prepare for the week ahead of you. You owe it to yourself and your success to sit with your agenda and review the week that has passed and the week that is to come. If you are going to take the time to do this, be brave enough to make the hard decisions associated with what you see ahead of you.

Let's say that in looking at your schedule for the week/grading period ahead, you notice that you will have no tests or major quizzes at the end of the week, but the following Monday you have two exams in core classes that you have found quite challenging. There are parties on both Friday night and Saturday night that you have been invited to. While attending both would likely be a great deal of fun and a chance to be with and enjoy your friends' company, a solid three hours of studying during one of those two evenings would make a world of difference on how well you do on the exams the following week. You must find a way to be brave enough to say to your friends, "I will definitely be there Saturday, but I have to study Friday night."

One of the key components of time management is organization. If you are the kind of student who struggles with organization, you will have to set aside more time and energy than most to find ways to methodize not only the work you are currently working on, but the work that lies ahead.

During my MFA—let me stop. I don't want you to be intimidated by any of the acronyms you will see in this book, so when you come to an abbreviation or word that perplexes you, feel free to revert back to the pages in the book dedicated to common terminology and acronyms associated with the college experience. You can also fall back on the study habits of an effective scholar, and simply look the word up in the dictionary or online—a professor of mine, Sherwin Bitsui, suggested all of the MFA candidates in the program should tack their creative manuscripts—which was one third of my thesis—onto our office walls. He went on to state that we should never delete or trash previous versions of a poem that had several revisions before the existing or current version of the poem.

Professor Bitsui suggested we place newer versions of poems directly on top of older versions. By holding on to previous versions of poems we might come to the conclusion that after review and reflection, the version of the poem that ended up being in the book was a combination of the second revision and the seventh revision. Seeing my poems along the walls of my office allowed me to see my manuscript grow in both length and depth. This also gave me the opportunity to move poems and see how they felt when placed in a different section of the book. What started as a simple piece of advice from a professor turned into one of the best techniques of staying organized and focused I could ever hope to employ as a writer trying to accomplish something complex and taxing.

Sometimes the simple act of focusing can help you manage your time more effectively. Focusing may take many forms, like having both a digital calendar on your phone or laptop and a physical one hanging in your room, both with due dates for assignments posted, can help you manage your time more effectively. Color code your calendar by class or time constraint. Leave a place on your calendar for notations or elaboration. Remember to take joy and pride in the act of crossing off an assignment or task on your calendar that has been completed.

Confession: I will tell you something that only my partner and my daughters know about me...I am the leader of an online alliance in the video game, Marvel: Contest of Champions. When I mentioned earlier in this book that I was a Merd... Mexican nerd...I was not employing hyperbole. But as committed to 60 Degree Wedge, Dementor, and DeezNutz as I am (I'm choosing to believe they really like cashews and are not being juvenile by the choice of this gamer name), I'm more committed to my students, my poems, and my writing process.

For this reason, I manage and prioritize my time because I know I only have so much of it in each day, in each week, in each semester, so I choose to make the most of it. In terms of prioritizing my time, with one being the most important and ten being the least important I place writing and reading at 2, just below spending time with my wife and daughters at 1. Helping my online alliance, The Revengers (again Merd), comes in at around 27.

QUESTION: how effective are you at managing your time between academics, athletics, social media, your actual in-person social life, work, your family, your chores, and all the other commitments you have? On a scale from one to ten with one being, "Miss...is it okay if I turn my research paper in one day early?" and ten being, "Wait...we had a research paper due today?", what number would you assign yourself? Regardless of which number you assign yourself, we could all use a little help with organization and time management.

There are so many techniques and tools you can use to manage your time wisely. Tangible things you can do to track what you are doing with your time, how you are doing it, and how you might feel while doing it are many times merely an arm's length away. Feel free to research time management apps on your smart phone that are equal parts student agenda and personal calendar with built in reminders.

I just typed the words "time management" into the search bar of my app store, and the following apps come up as free:

 Productive – Habit Tracker (4.6 stars)

A Tracker Time Tracker (4.6 stars)

Calendars by Readdle (4.7 stars)

Focus Keeper (4.8 stars)

Productivity – Daily Tasks (4.7 stars)

Schedule – Class Timetable (4.8 stars)

Focus – Time Manager (4.6 stars)

Focus To-Do (4.7 stars)

Daily Water (4.5 stars)

(Because a healthy student is a stronger student)

Flat Tomato – Time Management (4.6 stars) (Yes, this one has a crazy name but it is especially designed to help you avoid distractions that might make you less productive.)

Your phone also has a calendar that you can set reminders on for tests, projects, and assignment due dates. Thanks to technology, staying on top of assignments and their corresponding due dates is much easier for students today than it was say 20 to 30 years ago.

3. DEVELOP EFFECTIVE STUDY HABITS

The old saying is it takes 21 days to break an old habit and 21 days to form a new one. 21 days. Three weeks. That's it. So, don't be intimidated by the act of trying to form stronger study habits. In the same time it would take you to watch your favorite high school or college or NFL team play three consecutive football games, you could find yourself not only studying harder, but studying smarter. When working to develop more effective study habits, there are several things I want you to keep in mind.

STAY POSITIVE

Yes, studying—especially when reading or writing or researching a subject you don't find especially inspiring—can be hard work, but it can also be an opportunity to learn something new. As a scholar, we must all recognize learning as a thrilling and exhilarating experience.

Keep in mind that how you come to the act of studying matters too. If you are frustrated because of a relationship problem or the outcome of a football game, you will likely bring that frustration with you to the experience of studying. Create a buffer activity, take a walk, ride a bike, free read, play a video game for 15 minutes. Do anything that will allow you to breathe, relax, and approach the desk with a sense of wonder instead of frustration.

I have two daughters who are both astonishing scholars in their own right, but I had to work very hard not to compare the younger daughter to her sister, who earned a full ride academic scholarship to attend The University of North Texas. Good parents know to avoid the trap of comparing their two children. Excellent scholars also know to avoid the trap of comparison as well. Don't worry about how a sibling, friend, or classmate is doing in the course. You are a unique scholar with your own strengths and time constraints. Focus on yourself. In a moment, I'll write more about the dangers of distraction but for now, always remember that the most important scholar in your life is you.

LOCATION, LOCATION, LOCATION

Try not to study in a place filled with distractions. Studying in the living room during Monday Night Football while your father yells at the television screen as your two younger siblings argue over a video game, all while your mother is on the phone with her prima (cousin) is not going to be a space conducive to the learning process.

I'm one of those scholars who need silence to work and study effectively. If you are that kind of scholar, find a space that can be entirely yours. It could be your room, the den, a public library—just look for a space that is free of distractions and make that your go-to study spot. Some people love falling back on the quiet coffee shop. If that works for you, fine, but if you fear you may fall into the trap of people watching, the coffee shop may not work for you.

SILENCE/FOCUS IS GOLDEN

Even if you find the perfect space to study, you must avoid the trap of bringing too many distractions to your study space. Laptops and phones are powerful tools for research but with video games and social media they can also be an incredibly large time killer. What starts as, "Let me post one photo", can quickly turn into one hour lost in the cyber cloud of social media. Consider leaving your phone in your pocket or backpack, turning your notifications off, and setting your phone to vibrate or silent.

MAKE YOUR NOTES NOTEWORTHY

We are all different, which means we all process and learn information differently. With that being said, what works for one scholar may not work for another scholar when it comes to taking notes. Be aware that you may find yourself in a situation when you need to copy notes from someone else. Perhaps you are absent from a class due to illness, so you must rely on a study buddy for the notes from that day. Their note-taking style may not register with you in the same way, so after copying the notes, consider restructuring them to best fit your needs.

Cognitive psychologists call how we put similar information together in our minds "chunking." So, if it helps you absorb the material to say the words aloud as you note them, then by all means do that. This is an effective study technique because writing and speaking the words incorporates multiple senses into the study session and professionals believe the more you incorporate the senses the greater the chance of retention.

MAKE IT FUN

Sometimes using mnemonic devices—or a memory technique using word association—can help you remember material. In 5ᵗʰ grade, my science teacher taught me that the colors of the rainbow, which are also the colors of light moving through a prism spell out the name ROY G. BIV, or red, orange, yellow, green, blue, indigo, and violet. I have never forgotten that. It's just stuck in my brain for the rest of time. These word association games are powerful memorization techniques.

My daughters were especially fond of flash cards, and found joy even in the act of making them. There is such a sense of satisfaction that comes from sitting across a dining room table as someone quizzes you over your flash cards, and you get every answer correct.

WE'RE TALKING ABOUT PRACTICE

If there is no practice exam in your textbook, look for one online. You can even make up your own practice exam or ask another student in the class to make one for you. If you are part of a study group, you can all work together to make practice quizzes and exams for each other.

While practice may not make perfect, it definitely makes better, so the more you study the better chance you have of doing well on the quiz or exam. But be aware that there is such a thing as over-studying. Remember to take time for yourself. Free time and relaxation can be just as important to the successful scholar as study time.

A QUICK NOTE ON STUDY GROUPS

There were three of us. It was Scott Madison Frazier, Adam Chang, and I. We formed a club on our high school campus and called ourselves The 1600 Club, which at the time was a perfect score on the SAT. We formed study groups and while other students dropped in from time to time, we three were stalwarts. We each brought our own strengths to the table and we all grew as scholars because we were given the opportunity to be both scholar and teacher at some point during the study session.

I highly recommend you join or even better form a study group. Studying doesn't always have to be an isolated endeavor. Yes, there will be times when you need nothing and no one around to distract you from what you are studying, but always remember that sometimes just as with most things in life there is strength in numbers.

STICKTOITIVENESS IS KEY

Always keep in mind that studying is not something relegated to your spare time. No. Studying needs to be scheduled, put on your calendar, remembered and honored. Make a schedule, but be realistic. If you set aside Sunday evening as one of your prescribed study times, but find you cannot sleep Saturday night in anticipation of the Walking Dead Sunday evening, Sunday night may not be the way to go.

I have always found that I am a more effective and productive writer when I have a disciplined writing schedule. I truly believe that my success during my MFA was due in part to my rigorous writing schedule. I was able to find a writing schedule that worked for me, and I stuck to it at all costs. Find that schedule that works for you, and stick to it like glue.

TREAT YO' SELF

Just as it is important to work hard and study effectively, it is also important to take breaks. Remember to reward yourself with the occasional treat or downtime after putting in a vast amount of quality study time. Even treating yourself to a five-minute break after an hour of studying can go a long way toward breaking up the monotony of an uninterrupted, four-hour study session.

GOOD HEALTH PROMOTES GOOD STUDY HABITS

Believe me, as someone who accomplished his MFA while working full-time as a writer and touring workshop facilitator, living a healthy, balanced life as a scholar can be a challenge. There is no secret here. It's been written about time and time again. Exercise regularly—even walking everyday can provide you with great health benefits. Vitamins and herbs can also help you maintain a balanced life. Meditation and yoga may help you find peace and balance as well.

Just about everything written on the subject, however, will tell you it all starts with diet. Try as hard as possible to eat nutritious foods that are conducive to having what many consider a healthy diet. Yes it's okay to reward yourself with the occasional treat, but it should be just that—occasional. There is more I have to say about this in the coming section.

BE THE WELL-ROUNDED SCHOLAR

A well-rounded scholar realizes that effective study habits will help you succeed as a scholar, but they also realize that these study habits go hand-in-hand with work habits that take place in the classroom and on campus. Just as the well-rounded college scholar takes advantage of Office Hours a professor offers, the well-rounded high school student takes advantage of tutorial hours offered before or after school by the classroom teacher.

As a public high school English teacher for seven years, I was required to offer tutorials twice a week for one hour either before or after school so that students could make up quizzes and exams, they missed due to absences, or receive one-on-one help with a component of class they were struggling with. I offered nine one-hour tutorial sessions a week. Those tutorials fell every morning before first period Monday through Friday and every day after school Monday through Thursday. While many of those tutorial sessions were spent alone grading or lesson planning for the coming days and weeks, I can say without reservation that the students who came in to work with me during tutorials all showed success on the upcoming quiz, test, paper, or poem they were preparing for or working on.

Lastly, a habit every well-rounded scholar develops is the realization that one must note more than just what's written on the smart board. If you're only noting what's on the board and not what the teacher is lecturing about, you may find you are missing half of what you should be noting. In college, you may find you are missing 75 to 90 percent of what should be noted, as many professors in college rely heavily on lectures. I've often instructed young scholars to practice the craft of taking notes on their laptops by watching SportsCenter on television, but doing so with their laptop open before them. They must then keep their eyes on the screen while noting as much as they can about the stats or story being presented. Believe me when I say that taking notes on your laptop while listening to and observing a professor's lecture is a skill you must develop in high school so you can perfect it early in college.

THE ULTIMATE GOAL

Remember—we study at home or at a library or a coffee shop for the same reason we work hard to listen and take notes in class. We do so to learn. That's what all of this is for—so that we can become more effective thinkers and writers and people. While I do hope that you earn a high A on your next exam, what I hope more is that you learn a great deal, and that you can take what you've learned and grow from it.

4. HEALTHY BODY HEALTHY MIND

Keeping your mind sharp is essential in the learning process. One way we keep the mind sharp is to keep the body sharp. It is absolutely true that a healthy lifestyle not only makes living more manageable, it also makes learning more manageable. What follows are some healthy tips that every scholar should consider making a part of their life choices.

A HEALTHY DIET

Research healthy diets online and find one that works for you, or take parts of several diets and combine them into one that will be doable for you. The mind and body are connected. Neglect one, and the other feels neglected as well. As a scholar both in high school and in college, you will be pressed for time, but there are some simple life adjustments you can do to maintain a healthy diet that won't take much work at all. Remember what I wrote earlier about it taking 21 days to break and form habits. You can do this. You may already even be doing some or all of these. Below are ten simple things you can do as a scholar to maintain a healthy diet.

- *Drink water. Lots of water. According to the National Academies of Sciences, Engineering and Medicine, the recommended daily intake of water for a man is 15.5 cups or 3.7 liters, and 11.5 cups or 2.7 liters for a woman. It is the best thing you can do for your body and mind, so stay hydrated.*

- *When you order a coffee, order it with skim milk and skip the whip.*

- *Switch from white bread to 100% whole-wheat or whole-grain bread.*

- *Skip spreads on your sandwiches but if you must have one, choose mustard over mayo. Make a sandwich with a teaspoon of mustard instead of a tablespoon of mayonnaise helps you avoid not only 100* calories, but 11 grams of fat and 1.5 grams of saturated fat.

- Make your oatmeal with skim milk or 1% milk instead of water. By doing this, you add 6 grams of protein, which will help sustain you and prevent hunger.

- Add flaxseed to yogurt or smoothies. Adding two tablespoons of flax seed to yogurt or a smoothie adds four grams of fiber and 2.4 grams of healthy plant-based omega-3 fatty acids.

- Use spinach leaves in your salads instead of iceberg lettuce. Spinach leaves are much higher in omega-3, Vitamin A, Vitamin C, Vitamin E, and calcium.

- Drink unsweetened tea instead of sweet tea or soda. I have taken up the habit of adding a little Stevia to my unsweetened tea. Stevia is a zero-calorie plant based sweetener made from the stevia plant leaf. When adding any new thing into your diet be sure to do your research first. While Stevia is a zero-calorie option, some people have reported digestive problems due to Stevia consumption. If you are allergic to marigolds, daisies, or ragweed, you may also be allergic to Stevia as well. Be wise. Be careful. Be healthy.

- When dining out, consider trading the steak in for grilled fish. An eight-ounce T-bone with a 1/8th inch trim has 635 calories. A four-ounce grilled salmon filet has a little over 200 calories.

- When ordering a sandwich or entrée in the cafeteria or when making one at home, choose fresh fruit or fresh vegetables over French fries or chips. Doing so can shave almost 350 calories off a meal.

5. HOW TO RECOGNIZE AND AVOID THE TRAPS OF OVER-MULTITASKING

As a scholar, you will need to be well practiced at multitasking. In a class you may be charged to read silently while listening to a professor read aloud, all while taking notes over what is being presented. However, too much of anything is not healthy, so be wary of falling into the traps of overwhelming yourself by over-multitasking. What follows are some of the negative effects of over-multitasking.

1. *It can cause a weaker grasp on information being presented and learned.*

2. *Your ability to retain information may be affected.*

3. *Your stress and frustration levels may rise.*

4. *Sometimes the overwhelming feeling of what's called "brain drain" can occur.*

5. *It can lead to distractions, which may cause you to have to relearn material or redo a task done poorly.*

So, what are a few things you can do as a scholar to avoid the traps of over-multitasking? I'm glad you asked. What follows is a list of things you can do to put over-multitasking in your rear-view mirror.

- *Turn your cell phone to silent, vibrate, or off while studying or working on an assignment.*

- *Put away all distractions and anything that is not essential to what is being studied.*

- *Don't study in front of a television, and if you are not using a laptop while studying close it to avoid the traps of social media.*

- *Create and stick to a study or work schedule.*

- *If you're using your laptop disable or block all distracting websites.*

- *Remember there are only so many minutes in an hour, hours in a day, and days in a week, so use your time wisely.*

6. ACCENTUATE THE POSITIVE

On many occasions, I have told scholars to think of a quiz, test, exam, or paper as an opportunity for success. That simple phrasing gets you in the right frame of mind. In an ever-changing world, I know it's sometimes hard to maintain a positive attitude, but it has been said that positivity is a key to success. What follows are some things to remember about positive thinking.

- *Positivity attracts positive outcomes. The law of attraction states that like attracts like. So, stay positive and attract positivity into your life.*

- *Positivity helps relationships grow and remain harmonious. Trust me, I've been married longer than most of you have been alive. One sure way to ensure my partner, Aída, comes at me with hostility is to approach her with hostility. But when I give her a smile or compliment, she always reciprocates.*

- *Positivity helps you to make a great first impression. You only get one chance to do so, so always approach a professor, teacher, classmate, or anyone for that matter with a smile and sense of joy, and you will find down the line that the initial smile you gave them may have made all the difference in them bumping your 89.1 to a 90. Not always, but sometimes.*

- *Positivity promotes good health. The word disease actually means someone not being at ease. So when you feel joy, happiness, and positivity, you are actually helping your mind and body feel at ease, and in turn go out of its way to fight off illness and disease.*

- *Positivity combats stress. Positivity doesn't resolve stress entirely, but it takes your mind and body a step further away from negative thoughts and closer to peace.*

- *Positivity boosts motivation. Positive people tend to achieve their goals. That achievement increases their positivity, which in turn increases their desire and ability to reach more of their goals.*

- *Positivity creates opportunities. Negativity can blind you to the opportunities and experiences that exist around you. Start to see the glass as half full instead of half empty and you just may start to see that every problem around you has a solution. You are able to see that solution because your mind is open to the possibility.*

7. SET GOALS, BUT KEEP IT REAL

For several years, I was a member of the Dallas Poetry Slam Team that represented Dallas at state and national poetry slam competitions. The first year I made that team, our coaches, Roderick Rock Baby Goudy and Jonathan GNO White had us write three goals we had as professional performance poets both for ourselves and for our team down on a piece of paper. I wrote down the following three goals:

1. *Help my team, The Dallas Poetry Slam, make it to the Final Stage of the upcoming NPS and win the National Poetry Slam.*
2. *Win the Individual World Poetry Slam.*
3. *Win the European World Cup of Poetry Slam held in Paris, France.*

That same year, The Dallas Poetry Slam made it to the Final Stage of the National Poetry Slam. We placed third in the world and won the bronze medal. Two years later I won the Individual World Poetry Slam. Four years after writing those goals down, I won the European World Cup of Poetry Slam Championship held in Paris, France. I still have that small piece of paper that I wrote those original three goals on to this day.

Setting goals is an essential part of success, but remember to be realistic whether it's a short-term goal or a long-term goal. I knew I had the desire, energy, and time to commit to the task of being the best slam poet on the planet. Make sure you have the desire, time, and energy to achieve your goals. If you know they may be unrealistic, feel free to change them. Changing one's goals is not a sign of weakness, but a sign of strength. It shows you have an open mind and that you are courageous enough to change it. When setting your goals, keep the following in mind to remind you of the importance of goal setting.

1. *Goals give you something to strive for.*
2. *Goals make the impossible seem possible.*
3. *Goals teach us the importance of believing in ourselves.*
4. *Goals hold you accountable.*
5. *Goals help us know what is truly important to us.*
6. *Goals help us live, think, and feel more deeply.*

A LITTLE ELABORATION ON THE ACT AND SAT

There were three of us. It was Scott Madison Frazier, Adam Chang, and I. We formed a student club in high school called the 1600 Club, which was a perfect score on the SAT at the time. Other students would come and go, but Scott, Adam, and I were stalwarts. Some days we would meet in the library after school, other days we would find sanctuary in Mrs. Mallewick, our Pre-AP English III teacher's classroom. However, most days we would simply meet at someone's house after school. To be perfectly honest, since I didn't have a house, we would meet at either Scott or Adam's homes.

We all knew early in high school that a solid score on the SAT did not guarantee you would end up at the university of your choice, but we knew that we would have more opportunity for scholarships, and a higher chance of getting into the school of our dreams with a high score. We worked hard and pushed each other to strive for excellence. Each of us brought a different set of skills and knowledge to the equation. While I was quite good at writing, Scott and Adam were exceptional math students. We took practice tests together and offered each other peer edits of practice SAT written compositions. In the end, it paid off for all of us. We all did quite well, even better than we expected. This is the power of the study group. I hope as you approach your preparations for the ACT, SAT, or both that you will recognize and embrace that power.

Ultimately for all scholars, one of the culminating activities of your junior and senior year in high school will be to take either the ACT, SAT, or both. This can be an incredibly stressful time in a scholar's life, especially if you are a student who suffers from anxiety when facing a large test. However, there are some things you can do to prepare for this moment and hopefully decrease your stress level while increasing your actual test score.

1. ACT, SAT or Both?

Decide early on whether you'll take the ACT, SAT, or both. Once you have made that decision, you can begin focusing on what needs to be done to ensure success on the test(s).

2. Remember to Register Early

Football teams, baseball teams, soccer teams—they all rely on what they call the home court advantage. That's also something that effective ACT/SAT test takers do as well. Sometimes testing in a familiar site makes the test seem easier to tackle. How can you ensure that you get your preferred testing site? Register early. Look to register for these tests three months in advance.

3. Practice. Practice. Practice.

When taking a practice exam on your own, try to do so in a library or isolated testing site. Use a timer set for the exact testing time each section is allotted for the actual SAT or ACT. By placing yourself in a realistic practice-testing scenario, you are preparing both your mind and body for the stressors you will face on test day.

4. Develop the Right Study Schedule for You and Set Realistic Goals

After taking a practice test, you must be reflective. Look at the sections you struggled on and focus on those when studying. Be realistic when creating a study schedule and do what works best for you. For some of us, studying 30 minutes a day, five days a week is the ticket. For others, it's one hour a day, four days a week. Find a rhythm that works best for you.

When retesting a second or third time, think about the score you need to get into the college of your choice. Also think about what you realistically have time to accomplish. If you scored a 950 on the SAT the first time, consider setting 1100 or perhaps 1200 as your next goal instead of 1500 or 1600.

5. Focus When You Study

Do your research on the main components of the chosen test you are taking. Use online resources, as well as books you've checked out from a library or perhaps purchased to help you zoom in on those large sections of the test that you find especially challenging. You may find you need more study time set aside for the Math section compared to the Essay section.

6. If It's a Free Resource, Use It

Many high school campuses offer free practice tests such as the Pre-SAT. Some high school campuses offer vouchers for students who cannot afford to pay the fee associated with the ACT or SAT. Talk to your counselors and administrators to inquire about these vouchers. Keep in mind that checking out a book from a library and using an online test prep website are free. Some SAT/ACT test prep apps are also free. If there is a free study resource out there, seek it out and use it.

7. Continue Practicing

Go out of your way to take at least two practice tests (three if possible). The more you familiarize yourself with the test format, the better you will do. Some of the practice tests you can find online or in books actually use test questions that were taken directly from older versions of the ACT or SAT. Practice does not make perfect, but it sure does make better.

8. A Good night's Sleep and a Hearty Breakfast

People have been saying this for generations, and it still holds true to this day. You will succeed more with a good night's rest, and a growling stomach is a distraction for you and the scholars testing near you. So get a solid eight hours of sleep the night before the ACT or SAT, and eat a breakfast that will sustain you throughout the morning of testing.

9. Relax, and Don't Forget to Breathe

You can research relaxation techniques online. Experiment and find the one that works best for you. I've had scholars tell me the following technique works for them in alleviating stress before a big test:

1. *Take a deep breath and hold it.*

2. *Tense and tighten every muscle in your body for 5-10 seconds.*

3. *Relax every muscle as you slowly exhale.*

This is a 10-second relaxation technique that may work for you. Feel free to give it a try the next time you're faced with a stressful situation, whether it be a speech, test, or flight.

10. Fill in All the Bubbles

Remember—on both the ACT and the new version of the SAT, wrong answers do not count against you. You are only scored for the answers you get right. For this reason, as you notice time begin to slip away from you, go ahead and bubble in an answer for all the remaining questions, then continue working through the remaining questions, erasing and replacing with the correct answers as you progress through the end of the section.

11. Treat Yo' Self!

After taking the ACT or SAT, treat yourself to something small, like an ice cream cone or a movie. You've just accomplished something amazing and put yourself in the way of success. That success comes with hard work and hours upon hours of studying, so do something to celebrate you, and all the hours and energy you put into striving for excellence.

A LITTLE ELABORATION ON THE FACE-TO-FACE INTERVIEW

It's not always the case, but for some scholarships, a face-to-face interview will be requested. This may help the scholarship committee decide which of the finalists will be awarded the scholarship. As stressful at the scholarship essay can be, I realize that the thought of a face-to-face interview for a high school scholar can be even more stressful.

However, just as there are techniques we can employ to make our essay more compelling and creative, there are also things we can do to make the face-to-face interview another opportunity for success. As always, I like to fall back on advice from the experts. In my travels around the country, I take time to ask any high school or college scholars if there was a face-to-face interview involved in their scholarship application process. Then I ask if them if they have any advice they can offer younger scholars to help them prepare for the face-to-face interview. Below is the advice they have to offer you:

1. *Practice being interviewed by a fellow scholar, teacher, or family member.*

2. *Do not reply to questions with simply yes or no. They want to hear what you have to say, so elaborate.*

3. *Use inflections when speaking, and avoid sounding monotone.*

4. *Do your best to transform the moment from interview to conversation.*

5. *Before going into the interview, do some research on the scholarship. Find out how it was formed and a bit about its history. Knowing as much as you can about the history of the scholarship will give you a better way of speaking to how you are a good fit for it.*

6. *If you do not know the answer to a question the interviewers are asking, simply be honest about it. However, in that living breathing moment, feel free to elaborate on something you were speaking about earlier, or steer the conversation to something that you really want them to know about you or how you are a perfect candidate for the scholarship.*

7. *Remember not to focus only on yourself. Ask the interviewer engaging questions. Give them a chance to speak about not only the scholarship, but also about themselves. If the interviewer works in the field of study you hope to major in, take time to ask them questions about their career. If I was being interviewed by published, established poets for a creative writing scholarship, I would without question, find a moment in the interview to ask them, "What advice would you give an emerging poet?" The questions that you bring to the table turn it into a dialogue or conversation instead of an interview.*

8. *Make eye contact.*

9. *Have a solid handshake for the interviewers when you meet them.*

10. *That does not mean employ a Kung Fu grip of death while shaking their hand. Be firm and confident when shaking their hand, without being too firm.*

11. *If there are multiple people interviewing you, introduce yourself to each of them and try to engage and make eye contact with all of them at some point.*

12. *If there are multiple people interviewing you, but there is a clear leader in the room, give them a little more of your time and eye contact. If you were walking in to attempt to win the Dallas Maverick's Youth Scholarship, and Mark Cuban was, among the scholarship board, I would definitely advise you to make his both the first and last hand you shake as you enter and exit the room.*

13. *Sit up straight, stand up straight, and walk in and out with your chin up and a purposeful stride about you. Body language speaks volumes about you, in many cases, as much or more than the actual words you will say. Someone who walks in with a confident look about them already has an edge up on the person who walks in slouching without even saying a single word.*

14. *Speak at your natural pace, and employ your hands and other natural gestures when speaking. Emphasizing a point with an hand gesture or motion can be the most memorable moment of the interview.*

15. *After the interview, remember to follow up with a thank-you note. The thank-you note not only adds a personal touch, it reminds the scholarship board of just how thoughtful and polite you are. The thank-you note also allows you one last opportunity to say something about yourself that you did not get a chance to say in the interview.*

16. *Lastly, every single student I have spoken with about the face-to-face interview has always said the best advice they can give any scholar is to be yourself. You are a finalist at the point of the face-to-face interview. They already believe in you. By inviting you to be a part of the interview process, they are already letting you know that they find you impressive. Remember this. By this time, they know you as a scholar, but this is your chance to let them know you as a person. Don't you dare be too embarrassed to get emotional or laugh loudly in front of them. Having the courage to be yourself during the interview gives you the best chance possible of acing the interview.*

BE A PART OF YOUR CAMPUS

When you apply to any college or university, they will want to see that you are committed to the idea of being a part of your campus, and even being a leader on your campus. For this reason, you will need to be a part of student organizations, clubs, athletics, band, etc.

So many times, I'm confronted by students who say to me, "But Mr. Z, there's no club out there for me!" So, I'll ask them, "What do you like to do?" and they might reply, "Well, I really like playing chess at the park with my Abuelo." Then I will ask them, "Is there a chess club on your campus?" If they say yes, I challenge them to join. If they say no, I challenge them to create one.

The only thing that looks more impressive on a scholarship application than being a part of a club or student organization is founding one. If your school does not have one of the following clubs, consider forming one:

Poetry Slam Club

Literary Magazine Club

Gay Straight Alliance Club (GSA)

Shakespeare Club

Improv Club

Future Scientists Club

Pi Club (In this club, you discuss Pi and other mathematical concepts while eating pie!)

Creative Writing Club

Book Club

Anime Club

Chess Club

Video Games Club

Board Game Club

Democrats/Republicans/Independents Club

BE A PART OF YOUR COMMUNITY

When reviewing which scholars they are going to accept and offer scholarships to, most colleges and universities want to see that you are not only an extraordinary scholar but also an extraordinary citizen. They're looking to bring young men and women to their campus who recognize the importance of placing the needs of the community over their own needs at times. With that being said, you must be a part of your community.

How do you do that? By volunteering your time. Whether it's 30 minutes a week, 45 minutes a week, an hour a week, or two hours a week, find a way to give back to your community because that looks extraordinarily selfless on a college or scholarship application packet. What are some ways you can give back to the community? Consider doing one of the following:

Be a mentor to an elementary school student

Be a mentor to a middle school student

Be a mentor to an underclassman on your campus

Volunteer at a community recreation center

Volunteer at your community library

Volunteer at your local food bank

If there is no local food bank, form one

Check with local places of worship to see how you can donate your time

Volunteer at a local hospital

Volunteer at a local nursing home

Volunteer at the community senior center

Volunteer at a local animal shelter

Volunteer at a local museum

Volunteer with your area's Parks Department

Volunteer with any nonprofit organizations in the community

WRITING IT THE RIGHT WAY: HOW TO WRITE A WINNING SCHOLARSHIP ESSAY

The scholarship essay can be the difference between receiving a scholarship or not. It can be the difference between receiving a partial scholarship or a full scholarship. As a public high school English and creative writing teacher for seven years as well as a father of two daughters—one of whom received a full academic scholarship to the University of North Texas, the other a full academic scholarship to The University of New Mexico—I can honestly say that when it comes to the scholarship essay, you must work harder than you ever have on any essay in your academic career.

Let's look at a scholarship application essay that succeeds in so many ways.

Prompt 1: Some students have a background, identity, interest, or talent that is so meaningful they believe their application would be incomplete without it. If this sounds like you, then please share your story.

Managing to break free from my mother's grasp, I charged. With arms flailing and chubby legs fluttering beneath me, I was the ferocious two year old rampaging through Costco on a Saturday morning. My mother's eyes widened in horror as I jettisoned my churro; the cinnamon-sugar rocket gracefully sliced its way through the air while I continued my spree. I sprinted through the aisles, looking up in awe at the massive bulk products that towered over me. Overcome with wonder, I wanted to touch and taste, to stick my head into industrial-sized freezers, to explore every crevice. I was a conquistador, but rather than searching the land for El Dorado, I scoured aisles for free samples. Before inevitably being whisked away into a shopping cart, I scaled a mountain of plush toys and surveyed the expanse that lay before me: the kingdom of Costco.

Notorious for its over-sized portions and dollar-fifty hot dog combo, Costco is the apex of consumerism. From the days spent being toted around in a shopping cart to when I was finally tall enough to reach lofty sample trays, Costco has endured a steady presence throughout my life. As a veteran Costco shopper, I navigate the aisles of foodstuffs, thrusting the majority of my weight upon a generously filled shopping cart whose enormity juxtaposes my small frame. Over time, I've developed a habit of observing fellow patrons tote their carts piled with frozen burritos, cheese puffs, tubs of ice cream, and weight-loss supplements. Perusing the aisles gave me time to ponder. Who needs three pounds of sour cream? Was cultured yogurt any more well-mannered than its uncultured counterpart? Costco gave birth to my unfettered curiosity.

While enjoying an obligatory hot dog, I did not find myself thinking about the 'all beef' goodness that Costco boasted. I instead considered finitudes and infinitudes, unimagined uses for tubs of sour cream, the projectile motion of said tub when launched from an eighty-foot shelf or maybe when pushed from a speedy cart by a scrawny seventeen year old. I contemplated the philosophical: If there exists a thirty-three-ounce jar of Nutella, do we really have free will? I experienced a harsh physics lesson while observing a shopper who had no evident familiarity with inertia's workings.

With a cart filled to overflowing, she made her way towards the sloped exit, continuing to push and push while steadily losing control until the cart escaped her and went crashing into a concrete column, 52" plasma screen TV and all. Purchasing the yuletide hickory smoked ham inevitably led to a conversation between my father and me about Andrew Jackson's controversiality. There was no questioning Old Hickory's dedication; he was steadfast in his beliefs and pursuits—qualities I am compelled to admire, yet his morals were crooked. We both found the ham to be more likeable—and tender.

I adopted my exploratory skills, fine-tuned by Costco, towards my intellectual endeavors. Just as I sampled buffalo chicken dip or chocolate truffles, I probed the realms of history, dance and biology, all in pursuit of the ideal cart—one overflowing with theoretical situations and notions both silly and serious. I sampled calculus, cross-country running, scientific research, all of which are now household favorites. With cart in hand, I do what scares me; I absorb the warehouse that is the world. Whether it be through attempting aerial yoga, learning how to chart blackbody radiation using astronomical software, or dancing in front of hundreds of people, I am compelled to try any activity that interests me in the slightest.

My intense desire to know, to explore beyond the bounds of rational thought; this is what defines me. Costco fuels my insatiability and cultivates curiosity within me at a cellular level. Encoded to immerse myself in the unknown, I find it difficult to complacently accept the "what"; I want to hunt for the "whys" and dissect the "hows". In essence, I subsist on discovery.

Debrief: *Why is this essay so engaging? How does this essay make you feel? What was your favorite part of it, your least favorite part, if any? On a scale from one to ten with one being poor and 10 being excellent what number would you assign it and why?*

This essay was written by a high school senior, a Latinx scholar named Brittany Stinson. Not long after writing it, she learned that she was accepted into five Ivy League schools: Yale, Columbia, University of Pennsylvania, Dartmouth, and Cornell. She also found out that she got into Stanford, which is sometimes called the Ivy League of the West. Stanford at the time had an acceptance rate of 4.69%, a lower acceptance rate than any of the aforementioned Ivy League Schools. Stanford is where Brittany chose to take her talents.

This is what dedicating yourself to the idea of scholarship gives you—choices. When you complete high school after working absolutely as hard as you possibly can, I truly hope you find yourself in a situation where universities and colleges are competing with one another in an attempt to get you to select their campus as your future home for the next four years of your life.

Brittany is an exceptional student for sure, but that doesn't change the fact that this essay is just as exceptional as she is, and likely played a significant part of her being accepted to so many astonishing universities and winning as many scholarships as she did. This book, among other things, is designed to help you find successful ways to write an extraordinary scholarship essay.

THE SEVEN STEPS TO WRITING A SUCCESSFUL SCHOLARSHIP ESSAY

1. Know Who You Are Writing For

2. Pre-writing: Brainstorming/Listing/Proving to Yourself That You Have Something Significant to Say to the World

3. The Art of Introduction: How To Grab a Reader's Attention and Hold It

4. Nuts and Bolts: The Writing Process Throughout the Bulk of the Essay

5. It's Not Over When the Last Period is Typed: Revising, Editing and Proofreading

6. Two Heads Are Smarter Than One: Peer and Mentor Proofreading

7. Resources: Books, Campus, and Online Resources

1. KNOWING WHO YOUR AUDIENCE IS

Even students who are eager to throw themselves into the scholarship application process in relation to the essay portion fail to sometimes consider who they are writing to when answering their prompt. It is not always a scholarship committee made up of academics; sometimes the judging pool will be looking at your essay through a very specific set of eyes. For this reason, the student must be mindful of who is reading their essay, and ultimately who will decide whether or not you receive funding.

Keep in mind that the group that is reading your essay may be made up of mathematicians, scientists, artists, poets, or even generally educated people who don't specifically work in the field you are preparing to study, but are somehow linked to this scholarship. I've even seen judging panels made up simply of the mother and father of their child, a student who has passed away at a young age, and had a scholarship set up in their name by their family and community.

If you know who you are writing this essay for, you are more likely to use specific diction or word choice that the selection panel can relate to. Be mindful, so much so that you consider several things before putting pen to page or finger to keyboard:

(a) Who will be reading this? Where do they come from? What perspective might they look at this issue with? Do they come from the world of academia? Do they come to this moment from the professional world? Are they scientists? If so, what kind of diction should I consider employing or avoiding? Are they professors or are they simply community members who might appreciate it more if I simply wrote from the heart rather than the brain?

(b) Why does this scholarship exist? If this is a scholarship sponsored by Poetry Magazine, don't you think they will come to the prompt with different experiences than say, a scholarship sponsored by Green Peace?

Yes, you are writing your own personal truth, but keep in mind you are writing it to be read by someone or someone(s) different from you who come to this moment with their own experiences. Being able to see the prompt or issue from their perspective could help you in the long run.

Would you talk with your best friend, your brother or your father about poetry in the same manner you would when discussing it with a panel made up of poetry professors and poets? The answer is no. You have to be ready to tap into the language and images that would best resonate with the scholarship essay application review committee.

2. PRE-WRITING: BRAINSTORMING/LISTING/ PROVING TO YOURSELF THAT YOU HAVE SOMETHING SIGNIFICANT TO SAY TO THE WORLD

Quick Write Activity #1 20 In Less Than 20 (You will need 20 minutes for this activity, but if you need to take 30 minutes or even longer to fully invest yourself in this process, take the time that you need.)

So many times, when working with young writers, they tell me, "…but I don't have anything to write about." You must know that you have had 16, maybe 17 years of summers and winters in the particular part of the country that you have lived in, and that is an extraordinary fact. I'm certain those summers were filled with people and places that were vibrant, loud and worthy of being written about. I could talk with you about the power that resides in brainstorming and organized listing as pre-write activities, but I'd rather prove it to you with a quick write activity called:

20 In Less Than 20

In this activity you are going to come up with 20 topics for 20 different scholarship essays and you're going to do it all in less than 20 minutes. Let's begin. Get your stopwatch app ready on your phone. Go!

20 In Less Than 20:

Step 1: At the top of your page write down the word "People"

Step 2: Number down 1 through 5

Step 3: In the next 60 seconds, write down the names of five people that have had a significant impact on your life good or bad or a combination of both. Go:

_____

_____

_____

_____

_____

(Allow 60 seconds to write)

Step 4: Draw a hyphen or dash after each name. In 60 seconds, write down the first word or words that pops into your mind for each person. You can write down anywhere from one to 10 words; it can be a phrase or a short sentence. Go:

(Let's repeat with a slight variation)

Step 1: At the top of your page write down the word "Places"

Step 2: Number down 1 through 5

Step 3: In the next 60 seconds, write down the names of five places that you have either lived, visited, vacationed, broke down at, got taken to, dreamed of going to. Go:

_____

_____

_____

_____

_____

(Allow 60 seconds to write)

Step 4: Draw a hyphen or dash after each place. In 60 seconds, write down the first word or words that pops into your mind for each place. You can write down anywhere from one to 10 words; it can be a phrase or a short sentence. Go:

(Let's repeat with a slight variation)

Step 1: At the top of your page write down the word "Credo" (Remember, a credo is a short statement of belief)

Step 2: Number down 1 through 5

Step 3: In the next 60 seconds, write down the phrase, "I believe..." or "I believe in..." or a combination of both, then finish those thoughts by telling me five things you believe, five things that you believe in, or five things you believe to be true. (It's okay to write down that you believe in yourself. That's actually an extraordinary answer.) Go:

_____

_____

_____

_____

_____

(Allow 60 seconds to write)

(Let's repeat with a slight variation)

Step 1: At the top of your page write down the word "Someday..."

Step 2: Number down 1 through 5

Step 3: In the next 60 seconds, write down the word, "Someday..." followed by an ellipsis and then tell me five things you will do between today and the day that you die. Remember, it's okay to dream big. Go:

_____

_____

_____

_____

_____

(Allow 60 seconds to write)

If you managed to complete all 20 in less than 20 minutes, I'm entirely proud of you. But even if you only got seven really good answers, or 12, or 16, I'm also entirely proud of you. This is about quality, not quantity. The proof is right there in front of your face. You do, in fact, have something to say. In fact, you may find that you can thread a few of these subject matters together into one essay.

Just remember to have a central and focused theme. You don't have time to tell a handful of stories in one essay. Think about how a handful of these themes might weave through one moment of your life that then becomes a single essay. With some time, effort, and revision, any of these topics or themes could be transformed into an astonishing scholarship application essay.

3. THE ART OF INTRODUCTION: HOW TO GRAB A READER'S ATTENTION AND HOLD IT

Go back and read Brittany's opening paragraph to her scholarship essay. You have to go no further than the first sentence:

"Managing to break free from my mother's grasp, I charged."

It's active and passionate writing. Immediately I find myself wanting to charge with her. It grabs my attention and pulls me into the essay, which is what an effective introduction should do.

Here are some other things to consider when crafting your introduction:

There is nothing more intimidating in the writing process than looking at a blank computer screen. For this reason alone, the pre-writing phase is extremely important. Coming to the blank computer screen with notes, with ideas, with an outline could cause an introductory sentence to spark. You might find yourself coming to the blank computer screen with multiple opening sentences. If this sounds like a problem, believe me when I say, it is not. Having multiple opening sentences gives you the chance to look at them and examine them for their strengths and weaknesses. You might even find yourself morphing two or more of them into one astonishing opening sentence.

The same rule that I teach youth poets applies to students when writing scholarship application essays: two of the most important lines in the poem are the first and the last, and in essay writing, two of the most important sentences are the first and the last—with emphasis on the first.

NOTHING KILLS YOUR CHANCES LIKE A WEAK OPENING SENTENCE

"I'm writing you all to apply for the Eagle Scholar Scholarship" is an amazing way to ensure that they do not read another sentence of your essay. They know you want the scholarship; that's why your essay is in the pile. You don't have to state the obvious and the last thing you want to do, considering just how many essays they will be reading, is to make them feel as though your essay is a waste of their precious time.

You should also consider forgetting about "the stating my three arguments in one handy sentence method." Avoid anything that remotely sounds like the following: "I will begin this essay by stating why I deserve this scholarship, followed by a brief explanation of my family's struggle, concluding with a quote that exemplifies me." Sounds ridiculous, doesn't it? But trust me when I say, these kinds of opening sentences are out there and they drive the people reading them mad.

ADDRESS AND ANSWER THE PROMPT

Be clear, be definitive, be creative, but above all, read the prompt well and make sure that your opening sentence and your introductory paragraph are on topic.

If the prompt reads, "How might this grant affect your ability to study creative writing with a concentration in poetry?" the opening of your essay, your introductory paragraph and possibly your opening sentence should include something that sounds like, "With the Lannan Foundation Grant, I will be able to cover four semesters of tuition at the Institute of American Indian Arts."

KNOW WHEN TO SHOW/KNOW WHEN TO TELL

A good rule is to make your introduction clear and concise, no more than three to six sentences. But an effective essay writer will also strive to make the introduction as equally engaging and creative as it is clear and definitive.

It's not about bogging the reader down with detail after detail. It's also not about jumping immediately into the language of the brag. What it should do is address the prompt, and catch the attention of the readers in a way that sets it apart from the other essays waiting to be read.

There is a delicate balance that needs to be followed. Read and re-read your introductory paragraph many times. You do not have to have others read it and offer feedback before moving on, but it's not a bad idea to consider doing this—especially if you don't strongly feel that your introduction is equally engaging and definitive.

4. NUTS AND BOLTS: THE WRITING PROCESS THROUGHOUT THE BULK OF THE ESSAY

Keep in mind that knowing who your audience is and developing a strong opening sentence and introductory paragraph, while crucial to the overall scholarship essay process, is in no way the total means to an end. There is much work to be done. We still have a body that will support our thesis, and an ending that will leave them stunned.

"Delicate balance" is a term we will fall back on time and time again. While we want the body of the paper to be supported by interesting and engaging words, we don't want to show off our verbose, circumlocutory, and periphrastic vocabulary. (Are you still with me? I wouldn't blame you if you're not.) Big words can impress, but only when employed in a fashion that doesn't force the reader to consult their dictionary too often. Place these larger words into the body of your essay in a way that the context of their placement amplifies their meaning to the reader. Herein lies the delicate balance.

Keep in mind that some of the prompts you will be addressing will be extremely specific, while others will be broad and all encompassing. Be able to know when you have a bit more poetic license in your body, and when you need to remain focused and on topic.

Here are some writing tips you might find beneficial:

KNOW WHEN TO TELL/KNOW WHEN TO SHOW

Why on earth would you write something like, "I am an excellent poet who is quite good at working not only as an individual, but also in groups"?

There are so many ways to show this, rather than tell it. Consider using the following sentence instead, "During my junior year of high school, I was the managing editor of Pegaus, our school's literary magazine, but l also found time to organize a poetry slam for students once a month."

LISTEN TO TWAIN

Mark Twain once wrote, "I never write Metropolis for seven cents because I get the same price for city. I never write policeman because I can get the same money for cop." You want to speak at times, with elegance and sophistication in your essay, but you also want to sound like you. Be authentic. There is only one voice in the universe that sounds like yours, and that is an astonishing fact. Don't be afraid to write occasionally as you speak, as we speak.

BE CLEAR AND CONCISE

A centerpiece of your writing strategy should be finding the shortest, most direct and logical route to conveying your ideas. Get to the point.

Remember, however, that concise does not mean short. It means, no wasted words. If you can say it 550 words instead of 600, say it in 550.

WRITE PASSIONATELY AND IN AN ACTIVE VOICE

Don't "be motivated by" something; instead tell the readers that you find your inspiration in it, that you commit yourself to it. Using the active voice puts you and your actions at the center of an essay, making you an active agent rather than a passive recipient of your fate.

STATE YOUR ACCOMPLISHMENTS TACTFULLY

Don't just restate information from your resumé, but instead say why your accomplishments matter. Your academic achievements are useless unless you can convince your essay readers that they have given you transferable skills relevant to the task at hand.

Don't translate the line on your resume that says "Student Body President, Fall 2013 – Spring 2015" to "I was Student Body President for five semesters." Instead, tell your readers why that matters: "During my tenure as Student Body President at State University, I learned how to bring multiple stakeholders together around a table and facilitate a compromise."

5. IT'S NOT OVER WHEN THE LAST PERIOD IS TYPED: REVISING, EDITING AND PROOFREADING

For most of us this is the phase that tests our discipline. After hours, days, weeks, or even months of pouring all you've got into a scholarship application, it's time to tear up your essay. Remember, editing your own work is hard but entirely possible if you know what to do. It's the testing ground where many writers fall victim to despair and give up. Here are some tips on how to get through it with your mind and essay in tact:

REREAD YOUR ESSAY PROMPT AND ESSAY TOGETHER

Think of them as a Q&A session. Does your essay address and answer every part of the question, or does it sound more like a politician standing behind a podium? If your essay talks around rather than about your question, it needs rewriting.

REREAD EACH INDIVIDUAL SENTENCE

Ask yourself some questions about every statement you've made. Does this make sense? Does it logically follow the sentence that comes before it, and logically precede the sentence that comes after it? Does it relate to the topic of the paragraph and the overall argument of the paper?

READ IT ALOUD

I cannot begin to tell you what a powerful editing tool this is. Your final product should read like it was written by a knowledgeable and educated person, not a robot. Reading aloud can help you identify awkward sentence structures and unnatural phrases that should be edited or removed.

6. TWO HEADS ARE BETTER THAN ONE: PEER AND MENTOR PROOFREADING

GET A SECOND SET OF EYES

After proofreading your essay a second or third time, you may feel like your essay is good to go, but by now your eyes have gotten numb to the words and letters on the page and can no longer be trusted.

When it comes to catching grammar mistakes and typos, an editor can make a world of difference. It doesn't have to cost money either. Get a trusted friend or family member to read over and edit it.

They might find a "form" accidentally typed as a "from" where you missed it, or perhaps a common your/you're or there/their/they're mistake. Writing is an art, but when it comes to correcting grammar it's a technical skill too.

Next I offer you a checklist of questions to ask your essay once it has been written and proofread and revised. These aren't all the questions you should be asking your essay, but it's a great start.

Ask your essay the following questions once you have written it, read it aloud, proofread it, revised it, had a fellow student proofread it, revised it a second time, had a mentor proofread it, and revised yet again. (I never said writing a winning scholarship essay would be easy. In times of frustration or distress I ask you to fall back on my partner's favorite inspirational quote, "Nothing in life worth having comes easy."

JZ'S FAMOUS SCHOLARSHIP ESSAY CHECKLIST

_____ 1. Does the essay have an astonishing first sentence?

_____ 2. Does the essay have an active and passionate first verb?

_____ 3. Does the essay address the prompt?

_____ 4. Does the introduction engage the reader and pull them into the body of the essay?

_____ 5. Is the thesis clearly yet creatively stated (ideally in the first paragraph of the essay)?

_____ 6. How are the transitions between paragraphs? Does it read like one fluid essay and not a collection of four to six disconnected paragraphs?

_____ 7. Is the writing so effective that we come to root for you early and often?

_____ 8. Does the essay employ imagery and figurative language?

_____ 9. Does the essay employ impressive diction while maintaining the true voice of the speaker inside the essay?

_____ 10. Does the essay employ sentence variation?

_____ 11. Is there anything superfluous that can be cut or omitted?

_____ 12. Have you used formal language avoiding contractions (n't) unless they are being used to express a dialect or distinct voice being presented in the essay?

_____ 13. Are the sentences clear and concise?

_____ 14. Go back into the essay and underline or highlight all of the verbs. How many are simple linking or "be form" verbs (is, was, are, be, been, etc)? There should be as few as possible. If there are many, go back, revise, and work to make your verbs active and passionate. Remember, we impress readers with our verbs. The verb is the life force of the language. It's how we breathe and how we love. It's how we press the pencil down hard as we write, so as to leave an impression on things we were not intending to impress. The verb is ten times more important than the noun. 100 times more important than the adjective. (And don't get me started on adverbs.)

_____ 15. Has the essay been spell checked and grammar checked using the computer?

_____ 16. Have you read the essay aloud to check for voice, tone, and the overall fluid quality of the essay as well as any grammatical errors?

_____ 17. Have you had a fellow scholar proofread the essay for you?

_____ 18. Have you had a mentor proofread the essay for you?

_____ 19. Does the conclusion merely repeat what's presented in the introduction? It shouldn't. It should leave the reader breathless, simultaneously satisfied while yearning for more of your words and voice.

_____ 20. Does the essay have a gut-wrenching last sentence?

RESOURCES:
BOTH ON AND OFF CAMPUS

BOOKS AND SCHOOL RESOURCES:

1. The Ultimate Scholarship Book: Billions of Dollars in Scholarships, Grants and Prizes by Gen Tanabe and Kelly Tanabe

2. How to Go to College Almost for Free by Ben Kaplan

3. Peterson's Scholarships, Grants & Prizes

4. Confessions of a Scholarship Winner: The Secrets that Helped me Win $500,00 in Free Money for College – How You Can Too! By Kristina Ellis

5. Paying for College without Going Broke by Princeton Review and Kalman Chany

6. Scholarship Handbook by The College Board

7. The Financial Aid Handbook: Getting the Education You Want for the Price You Can Afford by Carol Stack and Ruth Vedvik

8. The Scholarship & Financial Aid Solution: How to Go to College for Next to Nothing with Short Cuts, Tricks and Tips from Start to Finish by Debra Lipphardt

9. How to Write a Winning Scholarship Essay: 30 Essays that Won Over $3 Million in Scholarships by Gen Tanabe and Kelly Tanabe

10. Your campus counselors, teachers, and administrators. Challenge your counselors, mentors, and teachers on campus with the following question, "What are three scholarships that are perfect for a student like me?" If they don't have an answer, be respectful and ask them to do some research and give you the answer in a week's time. Believe me when I say that they want to help you.

(Some of these books do not focus on scholarship writing, but they all have invaluable information and tools for scholars.)

ONLINE RESOURCES:

How extraordinary to be a scholar in this day and age! You have a world of resources in the palm of your hand. Don't believe me? Then open up your app store on your smart phone. Type the word *scholarship* into the search bar and watch how many apps come up. Many of these apps are astonishing, even going so far to allow you to copy your scholarship essay into the app to receive feedback and revision suggestions to make your essay more urgent and effective. Keep in mind that some of these apps are free, others cost money, while others have both free and pay-for-use versions that offer more services than their free version. But always remember you are a scholar, which means you should be concerned with studying and not earning money for scholarship apps, so reach out to that one tío or that one aunt who would gladly buy you a $3.99 app because after all, that's what uncles and tías are supposed to do. That's part of the job description.

Keep in mind while the app can sometimes cost you money, the website is almost always free to use. Here are ten websites to start searching for scholarship cash—along with an example of one scholarship from each to get you started.

Remember—the scholarship process is a living, breathing experience. Funding can be doubled or it can be cut completely as time passes. Some of the following scholarships may no longer have funding, while others may still be in play. Websites that are here today may be gone tomorrow. Be patient. Keep searching, and with time and research you will find the scholarships that are a good fit for you.

 ## 1. Zinch.com

Often considered a one-stop-shop for scholarship opportunities, Zinch is a place for scholars that are creative and inspired to find ways to get into college at little or no cost. It is often thought of as simple and fun to apply for and win. Create a username and a profile to apply for scholarships via Zinch. In this way, Zinch gets to know you and your needs to help you find the scholarship opportunities that are a perfect fit for you. The Weekly Three Sentence Essay Scholarship is one of Zinch's most popular opportunities, which also means it is one of its most competitive. Scholars applying are required to write a 280-character essay (which is shorter than most Facebook posts and not much longer than a couple of tweets) while competing for $1000 cash for college.

Visit Zinch.com for more scholarships.

2. Fastweb.com

If you're looking for another great and free resource with thousands of scholarship opportunities just a few keystrokes away, look no further than Fastweb. Among its other features Fastweb offers an expansive database of scholarship awards, career-planning information, and educational tools designed for students transitioning from high school to college. A while back, Fastweb offered the "Natural Disaster" PSA Video Contest, with a $3,000 scholarship awarded to a deserving undergrad scholar with both a passion for filmmaking and a desire to shed light on the impending consequences associated with natural disasters.

Visit Fastweb.com for more scholarships.

3. ScholarshipPoints.com

Much like how some online and physical storefronts offer customers a free gift after so many purchases, ScholarshipPoints offers scholars points for visiting their site and participating in different activities. This might include things like reading an online article, watching a vlog, taking a quiz, or playing a game online. Scholars who participate are eligible for monthly $1000 scholarships and quarterly $10,000 scholarship opportunities. Just remember scholars—you cannot begin earning points until you visit the site, so get busy earning those points.

Visit ScholarshipPoints.com for more scholarships.

4. Cappex.com

So many scholars I run into now tell me "Don't worry Mr. Z. I have a Cappex account, my counselor made me create one." Even though Cappex is one of the stalwarts that has been around a while, that does not mean it's not full of scholarship opportunities and financial aid advice. Cappex goes so far as to follow scholars into the college experience bumping up young scholars to their "College Pro" level, which then makes those scholars eligible to apply for the $2,500 College Pro exclusive scholarship. So, don't bail out on Cappex once you're accepted into a university. Stick with it and see what Cappex can do for you as an undergraduate college student as well.

5. Scholarships.com

With a name like Scholarships.com this site should be easy to remember. Rather than focusing only on scholarship opportunities, Scholarships.com also prides itself on being a site where scholars can find the perfect college for them. By focusing on major-specific scholarships this site is a great way to find universities that are actively seeking scholars with your interests and passions. A note for all the grammarians (or lovers of grammar) out there, the Proof-Reading.com Scholarship Program is closely connected with Scholarships.com. Yes, there is an essay required for this scholarship opportunity, but $1,500 for college would make it well worth the effort.

6. College Board Scholarship Search

The College Board Scholarship Search is a comprehensive site with one goal in mind—to place scholars on the path to financing our education. With well over 2000 online sources of financial aid and over 3 billion (yes, billion with a b) in scholarship awards offered, this search resource is worth a visit. A detailed questionnaire upon visiting the site will help the site better meet your financial aid and scholarship needs. While on the site, don't forget to check your eligibility for the Coca-Cola Community Colleges Academic Scholarship, which could offer select students $1,000-$2,000 in scholarship money if community college is part of your college path.

Visit the College Board for more scholarships.

7. NextStudent.com

This site was once called Scholarships101.com which shows you just how scholarship sites are a living breathing thing—sometimes changing names and at other times disappearing for a while, only to reemerge with a new name. This site's focus is on helping current undergrad college students pay for current and future tuition. Once you set up your user account with details about your major, minor, school year, and location the site strives to match you with scholarship opportunities designed for you. One recent undergrad was directed by NextStudent to the Stephen J. Brady STOP Hunger Scholarship, which is available to the winning scholar who has donated time and energy in the form of community service with a focus in the area of food service in the last 12 months.

Visit NextStudent.com for more scholarships.

8. StudentScholarships.org

Much like NextStudent.com StudentScholarships.org focuses on serving current undergrad scholars. It also prides itself on giving information and insights into particular fields of study and career paths, including expected salary after graduation. At StudentScholarships.org you can find out about the Dr. Aura-Lee A. and James Hobbs Pittenger American History Scholarship. This is an $8000 scholarship opportunity, with a payout of $2000 per year if you're a college scholar with a passion for and interest in American history and the government

Visit StudentScholarships.org for more scholarships.

9. ScholarshipExperts.com

ScholarshipExperts.com describes itself as fast, easy and free. All true. It's designed to help scholars make their way through the Internet in search of scholarship money during those trying undergraduate years. On this site, you will find the "Courage to Grow" scholarship. This is an opportunity for deserving undergrads to receive one $500 scholarship. The award is given out every month.

Visit ScholarshipExperts.com for more scholarships.

10. SuperCollege.com

A self-described database for scholarship opportunities, grants, and exciting contests for undergrad scholars, SuperCollege.com offers guides and helpful information on many aspects of the scholarship process including writing an effective scholarship essay and clever ways to save money for college. Weird as it may sound if you have a passion for both film and flashcards, SuperCollege may have a scholarship opportunity for you with their SuperCollege's Flashcard Scholarship, which comes with a $500 prize.

Visit SuperCollege.com for more scholarships.

And yet another bonus website:

11. collegeresourcenetwork.com

Another excellent site worth investigating is www.collegeresourcenetwork.com. They host an extensive database with thousands of scholarship opportunities totaling over $2.5 billion in college funding. It is considered one of the leading websites for scholarships designed for minority scholars.

Apps:

- *Plexuss College Application*

- *Scholly*

- *RaiseMe-College Scholarships*

- *Scholarships.com*

- *Apply.Me*

- *CollegeHunch*

- *College Scholarship Calculator*

- *Fastweb College Scholarships*

- *ScholarshipOwl*

- *Pocket Points Student Rewards*

- *Sallie Mae*

- *FieldLevel*

- *Goodwall: Jobs & Scholarships*

- *The College Fair*

- *Grandview C4 Scholarships*

- *FundforThought.com*

- *RIScholarships*

- *BeRecruited for iPhone*

- *Getting Into Scholarships*

- *Scoir*

- *College Interactive*

- *Achieve: Intern/Scholarships*

WRITE NOW: CULMINATING ESSAY WRITING ACTIVITIES

 Culminating Activity #1 Write Now

I want you to be well versed in what a common scholarship essay prompt looks like. What follows is a list of some of the most common scholarship essay prompts. If time permits, go back to the opening activity 20 in Less Than 20, and use it as a springboard of ideas to dive into writing one of the following common scholarship essay topics:

Academic Plan and Your Major or Chosen Field of Study

Sometimes the scholarship board simply wants to know why you are so passionate about your chosen major or field of study. Be prepared to write about how you came to be so passionate about Physics or English.

Samples:

> • *How will your study of _____ contribute to your immediate or long-range career plans?*
>
> • *Why do you want to be a _____?*
>
> • *Explain the importance of (your major) in today's society.*
>
> • *What do you think the industry of _____ will be like in the next 10 years?*
>
> • *What are the most important issues your field is facing today?*

Pressing Social Issues and Current Events

As someday college graduates, you are the future leaders that will eventually run the world. The committee may want to know what issues facing your community, your country, or your planet that you are passionate about. They may also seek to find out how familiar and up to date you are on current events and challenges facing the world today.

Samples:

> • *What do you consider to be the single most important societal*

problem, and why?

• If you had the authority to change your school in a positive way, what specific changes would you make?

• Pick a controversial problem on college campuses and suggest a solution.

• What do you see as the greatest threat to the environment today?

Awards, Accomplishments, Achievements

These essay prompts deal with the language of the brag. Remember to tread lightly, while you want to put as much metaphorical shine on yourself as possible, you don't want to sound obnoxious or self-centered.

Samples:

• Describe how you have demonstrated leadership ability both in and out of school.

• Discuss a special attribute or accomplishment that sets you apart.

• Describe your most meaningful achievements and how they relate to your field of study and your future goals.

• Why are you a good candidate to receive this award?

People and Places That Have Shaped You

Many times, scholarship boards will want to know where you come from and who the people are that have shaped you into the scholar you are today. Be prepared to write about your personal history, your background, and the people who have influenced and shaped you.

Samples:

• Pick an experience from your own life and explain how it has influenced your development.

• Who in your life has been your biggest influence and why?

• How has your family background affected the way you see the world?

• How has your education contributed to who you are today?

Your Future and Personal Short-Term and Long-Term Goals

Scholarship committees look for dreamers. They want to reward young people with aspirations. So have an answer ready for questions concerning your five and ten-year goals as well as what you hope to attain from your college experience.

Samples:

- *Briefly describe your long and short-term goals.*
- *Where do you see yourself 10 years from now?*
- *Why do you want to get a college education?*

Topics Simply Related to Your Financial Need

Sometimes one of the largest factors in determining which scholars will be awarded the scholarship comes down to which ones simply need it the most. While writing about your family's financial struggles can be challenging, be brave enough to be honest.

Samples:

- *From a financial standpoint, what impact would this scholarship have on your education?*
- *State any special personal or family circumstances affecting your need for financial assistance.*
- *How have you been financing your college education?*

Off the Beaten Path

Sometimes the scholarship board wants to know which scholars will be daring enough to choose a prompt that will allow more creativity in the writing. We read an essay by a scholar who chose to be daring enough to write about a trip to Costco and what it taught her about life. Let your writing be daring and odd, like you.

Samples:

- *Choose a person or persons you admire and explain why.*
- *Choose a book that has affected you deeply and explain why.*
- *Choose one moment from your life that explains to the world what work ethic means to you.*
- *Choose one moment from your life that defines who you are to the world. What about this moment defines you? What does this one moment say to the world about you?*

These are merely some of the most common questions. The most common questions change and mutate from year to year, but this list of categories and sample questions is a good tool for students to think about and be prepared to write about when the scholarship season arrives.

ONE FINAL READ

What follows is another successful scholarship essay. Let's read it and reflect.

Prompt 3: Who in your life has taught you the most about the idea of overcoming challenges? How did they do so? What impact have they had on how you tackle challenges both on and off campus? And how do you plan to face the challenges that lie ahead?

As an emigrant from the small and violence-ridden Central American nation of El Salvador, I've been raised with the expectation of succeeding in a land of opportunity. While growing up in the outskirts of Downtown LA in the neighborhood of Boyle Heights, I learned that the only way to escape my condition was to receive an education. The examples set forth by my family laid the foundation for my love of learning and motivated me to pursue a higher education through my pursuit of a better life I discovered a kindling passion for math and science that has driven me to seek a career as an engineer.

My parents sacrificed their time and energy to provide educational opportunities for me. When I arrived in the United States at the age of five, my father worked at a 99-cent store warehouse and my mother worked the graveyard shift at a shirt factory. Eventually, in search of a career, they began taking classes at a community college. It is my parents and their struggles that showed me the value of an education. My brother and sister have similarly followed this path of learning by excelling in school and gaining acceptance into a top tier university. My parents' focus on education motivated us to do well in school because they knew it was the only way that we could create our own path toward a better life. Thus, I set out on my path to a better life.

Confronting challenges head-on has been my signature attitude since I entered the American school system. Despite not being a native English speaker, I won third place in a school wide spelling bee in kindergarten and realized that my status as an immigrant did not mean I was any less capable of competing with those around me. I craved for a chance to challenge myself. This desire burned inside of me throughout my elementary school years—I competed in another spelling bee and made it to the local district level, I led a group of my peers in a district wide math competition where we took home three medals, and gained acceptance to a two-week residential summer science camp at the University of Southern

California.

Throughout my middle school years, I found that I was not challenged enough in school and upon realizing this, I sought a way to fulfill that desire that had been so dominant just a few years prior. Soon I found myself taking a 20-minute bus ride to attend a local community college course on Intermediate Algebra. The thought of having to wait for a bus didn't bother me because I enjoyed going to class every day, I enjoyed the idea of being on my own, and, most importantly, I enjoyed taking the initiative to seek out challenges.

My tendency to challenge myself academically grew during high school as I tackled higher-level science classes. After completing two years of chemistry, I realized it was time to tackle and master physics. I petitioned for the creation of an AP Physics course because I felt that an introductory physics course would not be enough to prepare me for college level physics. Thus far, the AP Physics class has been one of my greatest challenges and, despite the stress that it brings into my life, I am enjoying every minute of it. Because of my love for math and science, pursuing a career in a STEM field has long since been at the forefront of my attention. My family has always encouraged me to explore engineering and gladly helped pay for my trip to Stanford for a summer engineering camp despite having to go into debt to do so. I am grateful for the efforts my family has made because they have helped me reach a position where I am able to pursue a higher education.

Cesar Arevalo, a California-based high school student who fled El Salvador at age five, wrote this scholarship application essay. Because of his essay, grades, and work ethic, he was accepted into six Ivy League schools, four UCs, MIT, and Stanford.

Debrief: Why is this essay so engaging? How does this essay make you feel? What was your favorite part of it, or your least favorite part, if any? On a scale from one to ten with one being poor and 10 being excellent what number would you assign it and why? What changes could have been made to make it more engaging or creative?

Practice...Yes, We're talking About Practice

It doesn't make your writing perfect, but practice does make your writing stronger. Over the next several pages I am going to challenge you to write, then go back and review and revise. Think about the skill set you bring to the table. Think about all you have learned on writing an effective essay in your English classes. Think about your favorite writers and some of the effective stylistic techniques they employ. Lastly, think about all you have read, thought about, and learned from this book. Let's begin

You will be given three prompts, then room to write. Choose the one that you feel you have the most urgent and personal connection to, and write an essay that is a personal narrative that addresses the prompt while speaking about you not only as a scholar, but also as a person. Good luck. Write well.

Please choose one of the following three prompts and write it in the space provided for "prompt." Then begin writing the first of a few practice essays you will attempt to write:

1. *Describe how you have demonstrated leadership ability both in and out of school.*

2. *Discuss a special attribute or accomplishment that sets you apart from other candidates applying for this scholarship.*

3. *Describe your most meaningful achievements and how they relate to your field of study and your future goals.*

Prompt:

_____
_____
_____

Accompanying Essay:

_____
_____
_____
_____
_____
_____
_____
_____
_____
_____
_____
_____

REVISION CHALLENGE:

Look at the following opening paragraph to a personal narrative essay about a moment that changed my life as both a scholar and a person.

It was as if I was alone on a hike. How foolish it was to be out on a day like this, with temperatures well above 100 degrees. I blame him for my carelessness. I was less than a mile from the falls when I lost my footing and felt nothing, only gravity. My arms, far too thin for wings, went out wildly gesticulating but to no avail. The fall must have been no more than 12 feet but I landed with a dull thud on the large round boulder beneath me that had once been a foothold. I have felt pain before, but not like this. It was so close to the center of me, where the seventh rib meets the sternum. I know that something inside of me is broken, but it is too early to tell if it is flesh, bone, or something else. I close my eyes, and take a deep breath. The mountain evaporates, and all that is there before me is my open laptop and a Facebook message from a stranger who shares half of my blood that reads, "You don't know me, not really, and I hate to tell you like this but my father—I mean, our father is dead."

I like to advise students to count the number of words in each of the sentences in each of their paragraphs and then write those numbers down in one column. We do this to check for sentence variation. Let's do a sentence word count for my paragraph above. If I count the words in each sentence and list those numbers down in one column it would look like this:

1. 10
2. 18
3. 6
4. 19
5. 15
6. 30
7. 9
8. 16
9. 24
10. 9
11. 45

Now, as a writer of a personal narrative essay, I need to ask myself some questions about what I have just written:

1.   *This paragraph is eleven sentences long. The standard length for a paragraph is four to eight sentences. Is this paragraph too long? Can it be edited, or shortened as concerns the number of sentences in it? What would happen if it was six sentences in length instead of eleven?*

Answer: While it is a bit on the long side, I feel it does a good job of introducing the tension associated with the pain of finding out from a stranger that my father, a man who left my mother and me the year of my birth and never returned, had died. I also think it functions well in introducing the conceit of injuring oneself physically on a hike as it relates to the pain one would feel emotionally by finding out about their father's untimely death.

2.   *How diverse is the sentence variation, and are the sentences functioning well? Are the shorter sentences adding urgency and passion which shorter sentences are designed to do? Are the longer sentences adding tension and suspense which longer sentences are designed to do?*

Answer: I have a good mix of short, mid-length, and longer sentences, so there is evident sentence variation going on inside the paragraph. I feel some of the shorter sentences create a quick, staccato urgency, and there is an intentionality that comes with that. I feel that the two sentences that come in at 30 and 45 words in length create a breathlessness that one might associate with a hike or a trauma. The sentences appear to function well in terms of both structure and meaning.

Now examine the essay you just wrote. Do a word count for each sentence. Write those numbers in the lines provided. Consider marking the paragraphs in some way perhaps by placing a line between the numbers where one paragraph ends and another begins to check your paragraph length variation. Then evaluate your sentence variation. Does your list looks like this for a word count in the sentences making up your first paragraph?

    1. 11
    2. 13
    3. 12
    4. 10
    5. 9
    6. 14

If so, you need to add some sentence variation, as all of these sentences are about the same length. In the space provided, list your word count for each sentence:

1._____
2. _____
3. _____
4. _____
5. _____
6. _____
7. _____
8. _____
9. _____
10. _____
11. _____
12. _____
13. _____
14. _____
15. _____
16. _____
17. _____
18. _____
19. _____
20. _____
21. _____
22. _____
23. _____
24. _____
25. _____
26. _____
27. _____
28. _____
29. _____
30. _____
31. _____
32. _____

33. _____

34. _____

35. _____

36. _____

37. _____

38. _____

39. _____

40. _____

41. _____

42. _____

43. _____

44. _____

45. _____

46. _____

47. _____

48. _____

49. _____

50. _____

51. _____

52. _____

53. _____

54. _____

(If your essay is longer than 54 sentences, you may want to consider shortening it. A rule that applies to both poems and essays is as follows: the greater the concentration, the greater the impact.)

Please choose one of the following three prompts and write it in the space provided for "prompt." Then begin writing the second of a few practice essays you will attempt to write:

1. *Choose one moment from your life that explains to the world what work ethic means to you.*

2. *Choose a book that has affected you deeply and explain why.*

3. *Choose a person that you admire greatly, perhaps someone who taught you a great deal about the idea of leadership. Explain why you look up to them and what it was they taught you about leadership, and how they imparted that wisdom onto you.*

Prompt:

_____

_____

_____

Accompanying Essay:

_____

_____

_____

_____

_____

_____

_____

_____

_____

_____

_____

_____

_____

_____

_____

_____

_____

_____

_____

_____

_____

_____

_____

_____

_____

_____

_____

_____

_____

_____

_____

_____

_____

REVISION CHALLENGE:

Go back to the previous essay you just wrote and highlight the first verb in the first sentence with yellow. Then highlight the last verb in the last sentence with yellow. After doing this, go back and highlight all of the remaining verbs with a pink highlighter—every single verb. After doing all this, count how many common linking or be form verbs that you have in your paper. You know, verbs like *is, was, are, were, be,* etc. This simple form of verb cannot be in the first or last sentence. Those are the two most important sentences in the paper, which is why we highlight those verbs with a different color highlighter.

How many simple or common be form or isolated linking verbs did you find in your paper? If it's more than five, you must re-write. In fact, an even better rule is if it's more than three, you need to re-write. Keep in mind your verbs need to be active and passionate. If I've said it once I've said it one thousand times—the verb is the life force of the language. The verb is ten times more important than the noun. 100 times more important than the adjective. Prepositions, please…if you want to impress your readers, whether it's someone reading a poem you have written or a scholarship application board reading your personal statement, impress them with your verbs.

Please choose one of the following three prompts and write it in the space provided for "prompt." Then begin writing the third of a few practice essays you will attempt to write:

1. *Pick an experience from your own life and explain how it has influenced your development.*

2. *Who in your life has been your biggest influence and why?*

3. *Where do you see yourself 10 years from now?*

Prompt:

_____

_____

_____

Accompanying Essay:

_____

_____

_____

_____

_____

_____

REVISION CHALLENGE:

After writing this essay, read it aloud. Does it sound like your natural voice and tone? It should. Now, go back into the essay and find eight places where, using a thesaurus you can replace eight words with a synonym that, for whatever reason, makes that sentence or that part of the essay sound more interesting or urgent.

After replacing the eight words, go back and read the essay aloud again. Does it still sound like your natural voice and tonality? It should. If it doesn't, go back to those eight words and try again.

Now we're playing and working with diction or word choice. Remember—we can impress a scholarship application board with our word choice. Why write *threw* when you can write *jettison*? Why write *think* when you can write *ponder*? You never know—that one extra impressive word you employ could be the word that pushes your essay into the pile of finalists.

However, don't beat the reader up with massive words. At the end of the day (and at the end of the essay), this piece of writing should sound like you, not a thesaurus.

DOLLARS AND SENSE

What does a college education mean to you, in terms of lifetime earning possibilities? That's a great question. In 2017, after extensive research, the Bureau of Labor Statistics determined that on average, a weekly salary goes up significantly as the worker's level of education attained also goes up. Below is some of the information the BLS presented in 2017. (Two things to keep in mind when looking at this data: 1. When you see weekly salary, the BLS was using the median salary per educational level, not the maximum. 2. A Professional Degree is a professional doctorate degree, while a doctorate degree usually refers to a PhD. The difference is that a PhD focuses on research and evaluation of theory, while a professional doctorate degree focuses on applying that research toward practical problems. Think of it this way: someone with a doctorate might hold a PhD and be a professor of literature at a university. Conversely, someone who holds a professional doctorate degree might hold an M.D. and be a medical doctor.)

DEGREE EARNED	WEEKLY SALARY
Professional degree	$1,836
Doctorate degree	$1,743
Master's degree	$1,401
Bachelor's degree	$1,173
Associate's degree	$836
Some college, no degree	$774
High school diploma, no college	$712
Less than a high school diploma	$520

The study also found that surgeons, orthodontists, anesthesiologists, obstetricians, and psychiatrists were generally among the highest paid, making well over $200,000 a year. Near the top of the salary hierarchy were also dentists, nurse anesthetics, chief executives, pilots, flight engineers, and petroleum engineers who all made between $175,000-$200,000 a year on average. It went on to state that making well above a six figure salary included professions like attorneys, podiatrists, architectural and engineering managers, as well as financial managers.

I always fall back on the fact that a degree puts you in a situation where you may end up doing something that you love as a job or career. A job like that is priceless. One might make $40,000 a year doing something they absolutely love to do, while someone else might make $95,000 a year doing something they dread. While one might be wealthy in money, they might be poor in happiness. The other might measure their personal wealth by the joy they find in their job and the good it does for humanity. Who's to say who is the wealthier of the two?

The data we just looked at is startling to say the least, and there is more that I could say on the subject. However, rather than overwhelm you with pie charts and bar graphs, I thought I'd take a momentary break from this book, and simply tell you about my neighbor Paul.

MY NEIGHBOR PAUL

My neighbor Paul is a good-natured, 70-year old Jewish man that I am lucky to call a friend. You may be wondering what you have in common with a 70-year old Jewish retiree, but I imagine it is more than you think,

At one point in his life, my neighbor Paul was a young teenager like yourself with his entire life ahead of him. He attended community college after high school, but found that he excelled in partying more than anything else. He knew his life needed to change, but he also knew that when he decided to transfer from a community college to a university, the financial cost would increase dramatically.

He decided to make that change and work to help offset the cost of college by joining the military. He served four years in the Navy, and two years after that in the Reserves. He served as an engineer for the bulk of his time in the military. Upon leaving the military, he was able to take advantage of the GI Bill, which paid for a significant portion of his college tuition. He did have to take out some loans to help pay for graduate school, but not nearly as much as his other doctoral candidates.

When my neighbor Paul sat down and seriously thought about his future, he came to the conclusion that he wanted to find a job he would find fascinating, but would also be in incredibly high demand while still paying him a significant salary. For him, there was only one answer: dentist. "The world will always need dentists," he's quite fond of saying.

My neighbor Paul started out as a dentist working in an office that was actually owned by two other dentists. Eventually, he saved up enough money to get his own space and start his own practice in North Dallas. Keep in mind, my neighbor Paul worked in the late 70s, 80's, 90's and 00's. Salaries back then were not what they are today. For 28 years on average, my neighbor Paul made $85,000 a year. However, at age 56, he sold his practice to take a job at a prison in Jacksboro, Texas. At the time, the University of Texas, which my neighbor Paul is an alumnus of, was starting a program in which they would place dentists in prisons in Texas. The only services offered in the prison program would be cleanings, extractions, and fillings. My neighbor Paul says those are, without question, the easiest tasks associated with dentistry. Inmates would have to qualify with good behavior to be a part of the program, so Paul spent many hours simply waiting for patients to earn the right to visit him. He's told me many times that when he was caught up on paperwork and had no patients, he simply did crossword puzzles or read.

My neighbor Paul was a prison dentist for the last eight years of his professional career. He only had to work four days a week instead of five. His salary was set at $116,000 a year. At the time, he was actually making more money to do less work, while not having to fight through the headaches of trying to receive payments from delinquent insurance companies.

Another reason my neighbor Paul decided to take the job as prison dentist was because for the last eight years of his career, he was a staff member of the University of Texas, since this program was actually their design. To receive a TRS (Teacher Retirement System) package from the University of Texas, one must work at least five years. When he retired, he earned enough time in the program to receive $1,500 a month in retirement for the rest of his life, on top of what he would receive from Social Security. My neighbor Paul retired at age 62.

So, let's look at some data surrounding the life of my neighbor Paul:

YEARS OF WORK	SALARY PER YEAR	TOTAL MONEY EARNED
1975-2003	$85,000	$2,380,000
2003-2011	$116,000	$928,000

The total lifetime earnings for my neighbor Paul: $3,308,000

My neighbor Paul actually owns two homes in the greater Dallas area. Both are paid off in full, and have been for a very long time. My neighbor Paul owns two cars (SUVs); both were paid for in cash and never required a car payment. He holds no credit card debt, and no student loan debt, as he paid them off almost immediately after becoming a dentist.

All of the money he has in stocks, bonds, CDs, personal investments and holding accounts grows with every passing day. You can reach a point in life where instead of working for your money, your money works for you. My neighbor Paul has reached that point. He and his wife travel several times a year. They eat out more than they eat at home. For the last eight years, while I have been working as a poet, writer, and teacher, I have seen him on his porch playing with a Rubik's cube, reading, playing chess against his computer, or doing whatever he wants to do. Because he can.

My neighbor Paul has an extraordinary life. If you ask him, he will say it is all due to his professional doctorate degree, which he earned those many years ago when he was not much older than you are now.

Where you will be 45 years from now is a very perplexing thing to ponder, and I know as a young scholar it's hard to wrap your head around where you will be at that time. I hope wherever you find yourself then, you will be a homeowner with no debt, with two new cars that you own outright, and a lovely partner who has worked just as hard as you have. Look when it's all said and done, someone has to be filthy, stinking rich; someone has to be fulfilled and happy; someone has to be a multi-millionaire. It might as well be my neighbor Paul...or you.

One of the ways you can work toward that future is through the act of scholarship. As we approach the end of this book, I want to give you a few scholarships specific to certain kinds of students, and then a longer index of scholarships, in which one of the qualifying factors is simply the state in which you reside.

There is a wealth of scholarships out there for you, and there is no limit on how many you can apply to. If you want to apply to 10, 20, 30...go for it. Will it be time-consuming and challenging? Yes.

I once had a student say to me, "Mr. Z, what if I apply for 25 scholarships and I only get nine? Would it be worth it?" I replied, "Okay let's assume the first one was for $75, the second one was for $250, and the third one was for $475. Both the fourth and fifth were for $500 each, and the sixth, seventh, eighth, and ninth were all over $1000 each." I then asked the scholar to add all those numbers up. When they did, they were astonished. It will take research and work, but I'll get you started here with a handful of scholarships that might be a good fit for you.

5 SCHOLARSHIPS FOR STUDENTS WHO IDENTIFY AS STUDENTS OF COLOR

1. **Actuarial Diversity Scholarship**

    Deadline: May 1
    Website: actuarialfoundation.org/programs

2. **AICPA Fellowships for Minority Doctoral Students**

    Deadline: May 15
    Website: aicpa.org

3. **CBC Education Scholarship**

    Deadline: May 19
    Website: cbcfinc.academicworks.com

4. **Hyatt Hotels Fund for Minority Lodging Management Students**

    Deadline: May 1
    Website: ahlef.org

5. **William A. Crawford Minority Teacher Scholarship**

    Deadline: September 4
    Website: in.gov

5 SCHOLARSHIPS FOR STUDENTS WHO IDENTIFY AS LATINX

1. **Ronald McDonald House Charities/HACER Scholarship**

   Deadline: See website
   Website: usascholarships.com

2. **NBCUniversal/LNESC Scholarship**

   Deadline: July 22
   Website: Lnesc.org

3. **Society of Hispanic Professional Engineers (SHPE) Foundation Scholarship**

   Deadline: See website
   Website: chcinextopp.net

4. **La Unidad Latina Foundation**

   Deadline: October
   Website: lulf.org

5. **Association of Latino Professionals for America (ALPFA) Scholarship**

   Deadline: See website
   Website: https://alpfa.fluidreview.com

5 SCHOLARSHIPS FOR STUDENTS WHO IDENTIFY AS WOMEN

1. **Linda Lael Miller Scholarship**

   Deadline: See website
   Website: lindalaelmiller.com

2. **Jeanette Rankin Foundation Scholarship**

   Deadline: See website
   Website: open only during application process

3. **U.S. Army Women's Foundation Legacy Scholarships**

   Deadline: See website
   Website: Search USAWF Legacy Scholarship

4. **American Association of University Women Scholarship**

   Deadline: See website
   Website: AAUW Website

5. **Mr. and Mrs. Spencer T. Olin Fellowship for Women in Graduate Study**

   Deadline: See website
   Website: Search Olin Fellowship online

5 SCHOLARSHIPS FOR STUDENTS WHO IDENTIFY AS BLACK OR AFRICAN AMERICAN

1. **Martin Luther King Scholarship Award**

   Deadline: June 1
   Website: aca.org

2. **CBC Spouses Education Scholarship**

   Deadline: May 18
   Website: cbcfincacademicworks.com

3. **CBC Spouses Performing Arts Scholarship**

   Deadline: April 20
   Website: cbcfinc.academicworks.com

4. **CBC Spouses Visual Arts Scholarship**

   Deadline: April 20
   Website: cbcfinc.academicworks.com

5. **Black History Month Contest**

   Deadline: See website
   Website: floridablackhistory.com

5 SCHOLARSHIPS FOR STUDENTS WHO IDENIFY AS ASIAN AMERICAN

1. **Indian American Scholarship**

   Deadline: See website
   Website: www.upakarfoundation.org

2. **The EDSA Minority Scholarship**

   Deadline: May 18
   Website: https://lafoundation.org/scholarship/scholarships-and-fellowships/awards-avsailable/

3. **Bureau of Indian Education Higher Education Grant Program**

   Deadline: June 1
   Website: consultation@bia.gov

4. **NABA National Scholarship**

   Deadline: January 31
   Website: www.nabainc.org

5. **STEM Bridge Scholarship**

   Deadline: See website
   Website: www.vsgc.odu.edu

5 SCHOLARSHIPS FOR STUDENTS WHO IDENTIFY AS NATIVE AMERICAN OR FIRST NATIONS

1. **Albuquerque Community Foundation (ACF) Notah Begay III Scholarship**

   Deadline: March 6
   Contact: nancy@albuquerquefoundation.org

2. **American Indian College Fund Full Circle Scholarship Program**

   Deadline: May 31
   Website: scholarships@collegefund.org

3. **American Indian Nurse Scholarship Awards**

   Deadline: December 1
   Website: nscda-ma@verizon.net

4. **Bureau of Indian Education Higher Education Grant Program**

   Deadline: June 1
   Website: consultation@bia.gov

5. **Cheyenne and Arapaho Higher Education Grants**

   Deadline: June 1 and November 1
   Website: cheyenneandarapaho-nsn.gov

5 SCHOLARSHIPS FOR STUDENTS WHO IDENTIFY AS LGBTQUIA

1. **Point Foundation LGBTQ Scholarship**

   Deadline: Late January
   Website: pointfoundation.org

2. **Parents, Families, and Friends of Lesbians and Gays (PFLAG) Scholarships**

   Deadline: April 2
   Website: pflag.org

3. **League Foundation LGBTQ Scholarship**

   Deadline: April 15
   Website: leaguefoundation.org

4. **Gamma Mu Foundation Scholarships**

   Deadline: March 31
   Website: gammamufoundation.org

5. **Queer Foundation Queer Scholars Program**

   Deadline: February 14
   Website: queerfoundation.org

5 SCHOLARSHIPS FOR STUDENTS WHO IDENTIFY AS JEWISH

1. **Jewish War Veterans of the United States of America Bernard Rotberg Memorial Scholarship**

   Deadline: May 1
   Website: www.jwv.org

2. **Leon Brooks Memorial Grant**

   Deadline: May 30
   Website: www.jwv.org

3. **Charles Kosmutza Memorial Grant**

   Deadline: May 30
   Website: www.jwv.org

4. **Max R. & Irene Rubenstein Memorial Grant**

   Deadline: May 30
   Website: www.jwv.org

5. **Seymour and Phyllis Shore Memorial Grant**

   Deadline: May 1
   Website: www.jwv.org

5 SCHOLARSHIPS FOR STUDENTS WHO IDENIFY AS ALASKAN NATIVE

1. **American Meteorological Society/Industry Minority Scholarship**

   Deadline: May 1
   Website: www.ametsoc.org

2. **Box Engineering Diversity Scholarship**

   Deadline: October 30
   Website: www.boxdiversityscholarship.com/

3. **Full Circle/TCU Scholarship Program**

   Deadline: May 31
   Website: http://collegefund.org

4. **Intel Scholarship**

   Deadline: mid-May
   Website: www.aises.org/scholarships

5. **Weisman Scholarship**

   Deadline: See website
   Website: www.ctohe.org

5 SCHOLARSHIPS FOR STUDENTS WHO IDENIFY AS NATIVE HAWAIIN / PACIFIC ISLANDER

1. **Ambassador Minerva Jean Falcon Hawaii Scholarship**

   Deadline: February 15
   Website: www.hawaiicommunityfoundation.org

2. **Asian Women In Business Scholarship**

   Deadline: See website
   Website: www.awib.org/index.cfm?fuseaction=Page.viewPage&pageId=811

3. **A.T. Anderson Memorial Scholarship**

   Deadline: mid-May
   Website: www.aises.org/scholarships

4. **Blossom Kalama Evans Memorial Scholarship**

   Deadline: February 15
   Website: www.hawaiicommunityfoundation.org

5. **Ka'iulani Home for Girls Trust Scholarship**

   Deadline: February 15
   Website: www.hawaiicommunityfoundation.org

5 SCHOLARSHIPS FOR UNDOCUMENTED STUDENTS

1. **Ascend Educational Fund Scholarships**

   Deadline: February 2
   Website: ascendfundny.org

2. **Association of Raza Educators Scholarship**

   Deadline: March 10
   Contact: aresandiego94@gmail.com

3. **Cofem Mexican-American Dream Scholarship**

   Deadline: September 30
   Website: scholarship@cofem.org

4. **Deferred Action San Francisco Fellowship**

   Deadline: April 16
   Website: civic.engagement@sfgov.org

5. **Esperanza Education Fund Scholarships**

   Deadline: April 1
   Website: scholarship@esperanzafunbd.org

SCHOLARSHIP OPPORTUNTIES BY STATE

SCHOLARSHIP	AMOUNT	DEADLINE
ALABAMA		
Alabama Education Grant	$1,200	See website
Alabama GI Dependents' Program	Full Tuition	None
Alabama National Guard Education Assistance Program	$25-$1,000	See website
Alabama Student Assistance Program	$300-$3,500	See website
Alabama Scholarship for Dependents of Blind Parents	Full Tuition	July 31
ALASKA		
Alaska Education Grant	$500-$3,000	June 30
Alaska Performance Scholarship	$2,378-$4,755	June 30
American Legion Alaska Auxiliary Scholarship	$1,500	March 15
American Legion Alaska Oratorical Contest	$1,000-$3,000	See website
Cady McDonnell Memorial Scholarship	$1,000	See website
ARIZONA		
Active Renter Property Management Entrepreneur	$1,000	April 1
American Legion Arizona Oratorical Contest	$500-$1,500	January 1
Animal Health International Scholarship	$1,000	February 1
Husband and Wife Law Team Arizona Scholarship	$1,000	April 17
Horatio Alger Arizona Scholarship	$6,000	October 25
ARKANSAS		
Arkansas Academic Challenge Scholarship	$2,000-$5,000	June1
Arkansas Governor's Scholars Program	$10,000	February 1
Arkansas Law Enforcement Officer's Dependent Scholarship	Full Tuition	June 1
Arkansas Military Dependents Scholarship Program	Full Tuition	June 1

Dana Campbell Memorial Scholarship	$2,000	May 15

CALIFORNIA

California Child Development Grant Program (100 scholarships awarded totaling $277,000)	$1,000-$2,000	See website
California Farm Bureau Scholarship	$165,750	March 1
California Law Enforcement Personnel Dependents Grant Program (LEPD)	$100-$12,192	February 1
California Teachers Association Martin Luther King, Jr., Memorial Scholarship	$4,000	February 17
California's Distinguished Young Woman Competition	See website	See website

COLORADO

Colorado Student Grant	$69,381,910	See website
Colorado Council Volunteerism and Community Service Scholarship	$1,500	January 30
Colorado Masons Scholarship	$7,000	March 15
Colorado Society of CPAs General Scholarship	$2,500	June 1
Zinda Law Group Scholarship	$1,000	December 1

CONNECTICUT

Connecticut Building Congress Scholarship Fund	$500-$2,000	March 10
Connecticut Aid to Dependents of Deceased/POW/MIA Veterans	$800	See website
Connecticut Minority Teacher Incentive Grant	$2,500-$5,000	October 1
Connecticut Tuition Waiver for Senior Citizens	Full Tuition	See website
Roberta B. Willis Scholarship – Need Based Award	$500-$4,500	See website

DELAWARE

B. Bradford Barnes Scholarship	Full Tuition	See website
Charles L. Hebner Memorial Scholarship	Full Tuition	See website
Delaware Educational Benefits for Children of Deceased Veterans and Others	Full Tuition	See website
Delaware Scholarship Incentive Program	$700-$2,200	See website
Diamond State Scholarship	$1,250	See website

DISTRICT OF COLUMBIA

American Legion District of Columbia Oratorical Contest	$100-$800	See website
DC Tuition Assistance Grant Program (DCTAG)	$2,500-$10,000	See website
Denny's Hungry for Education Scholarship	$1,000	September 15
Diverse Minds Writing Challenge	$1,000-$5,000	See website
Horatio Alger District of Columbia and Virginia Scholarship Program	$6,000	October 25

FLORIDA

ABLE Grant Program	Varies	See website
Florida Bright Futures Scholarship Program	Varies	See website
Florida First Generation Matching Grant Program	Varies	See website
Florida Scholarship Program	Varies	April 15
Florida Scholarships for Children and Spouses of Deceased or Disabled Veterans	Varies	April 1

GEORGIA

Georgia Hope Grant – GED Recipient	$1,801,678	See website
Georgia Student Finance Commission Public Safety Memorial Grant	$18,000	See website
The 5 Strong Scholarship Foundation	$6,000-$10,000	December 20
NASA Space Grant Georgia Fellowship Program	Varies	See website
Horatio Alger Georgia Scholarship	$6,000	October 25

HAWAII

Hawaii GEAR UP Scholars Program	Varies	February 15
Hawaii Pacific Gerontological Society Nursing Scholarship Fund	Varies	February 15
Hawaii Pizza Hut Scholarship Fund	Varies	February 15
Oscar and Rosetta Fish Fund	Varies	February 15
Ouida Mundy Hill Memorial Fund	Varies	February 15

IDAHO

Idaho GEAR UP Scholarship	Varies	February 15
Idaho Governor's Cup Scholarship	$3,000	February 15
Idaho Opportunity Scholarship	$3,000	March 1
Idaho State Board of Education Armed Forces and Public Safety Officer Dependent Scholarship	Full Tuition	February 15
The Mary Lou Brown Scholarship	$2,500	January 31

ILLINOIS

Illinois MIA/POW Scholarship	Full Tuition	See website
Illinois Grant Program for Dependents of Correctional Officers	Full Tuition	October1
Illinois Special Education Teacher Tuition Waiver	Full Tuition	March 1
Illinois Veteran Grant Program (IVG)	Full Tuition	See website
Minority Teachers of Illinois Scholarship	$5,000	March 1

INDIANA

Frank O'Bannon Grant	$196,838,902	March 10
Indiana Minority Teacher & Special Education	$1,000-$4,000	See website

Services Scholarship

Indiana National Guard Supplemental Grant	Full Tuition	March 10
Indiana Twenty-First Century Scholars Program	$22,787,104	July 1
The Mitch Daniels Early Graduation Scholarship	$4,000	See website

IOWA

All Iowa Opportunity Scholarship	$8,118	March 1
Governor Terry E. Branstad Iowa State Fair Scholarship	$500-$5,000	March 1
Iowa Barber and Cosmetology Arts and Sciences Tuition Grant	$1,200	July 1
Iowa Grant	$1000	See website
Iowa Tuition Grant	$6,000	July 1

KANSAS

Kansas Ethnic Minority Scholarship	$1,850	May 1
Kansas Military Service Scholarship	Full Tuition	May 1
Kansas Nursing Service Scholarship	$2,500-$3,500	May 1
Kansas ROTC Service Scholarship	$1,650 (on average)	May 1
Kansas State Scholarship	$1,000	May 1

KENTUCKY

Kentucky College Access Program Grant	$50-$1,900	See website
Kentucky Early Childhood Development Scholarship	$1,800	July 15
Kentucky Go Higher Grant	$1,000	See website
Kentucky Teacher Scholarship	$300-$5,000	May 1
Kentucky Tuition Grant	$200-$3,000	See website

LOUISIANA

Louisiana Go Grants	$300-$3,000	See website
Louisiana Rockefeller Wildlife Scholarship	$2,000-$3,000	July 1
Louisiana Taylor Opportunity Program for Students	Full Tuition	July 1
Louisiana TOPS Tech Early Start Program	$600	See website
Louisiana TOPS Tech Program	Full Tuition	July 1

MAINE

Maine Veterans Services Dependents Educational Benefits	Full Tuition	See website
Maine Innkeepers Association Scholarship	$500-$3,000	April 4
Maine Metal Products Association Scholarship	$100-$1,000	April 31
Maine Society of Professional Engineers Scholarship	$2,500	March 1
Maine State Society of Washington, DC Foundation Scholarship Program	$1,000	March 15

MARYLAND

Edward T. Conroy Memorial Scholarship Program	Varies	July 15
Howard P. Rawlings Guaranteed Access Grant	$400-$16,100	March 1
Maryland Delegate Scholarship	$200-$19,000	March 1
Maryland Educational Assistance Grant	$400-$3,000	March 1
Maryland Jack F. Tolbert Memorial Grant	$500	March 1

MASSACHUSETTS

Incentive Program for Aspiring Teachers	Full Tuition	See website
John and Abigail Adams Scholarship	Varies	See website
Massachusetts Cash Grant Program	Varies	See website
Massachusetts Christian A. Herter Memorial Scholarship Program	$15,000	February 6
Massachusetts Gilbert Matching Student Grant	$200-$2,500	See website

MICHIGAN

Michigan Tuition Grant (22,000 students awarded over 30 million dollars)	$1,524	July 1
Michigan Tuition Incentive Program	$34,600,000	See website
Michigan Society of Professional Engineers Scholarship For High School Seniors	Varies	See website
Midwest Student Exchange Program	Varies	See website
American Legion Michigan Auxiliary Memorial Scholarship	$500	March 15

MINNESOTA

Minnesota Educational Assistance for Veterans	$750	See website
Minnesota Child Care Grant	$2,800	See website
Minnesota Indian Scholarship Program	$6,000	See website
Minnesota Public Safety Officers Survivors Grant	$5,808-$13,000	See website
Minnesota State Grant Program	$100-$10,745	See website

MISSISSIPPI

Mississippi Eminent Scholars Grant	$2,500	September 15
Mississippi Higher Education Legislative Plan	Full Tuition	March 31
Mississippi Tuition Assistance Grant	$500-$1,000	September 15
Nissan Scholarship	Full Tuition	March 1
Gulf Coast Hurricane Scholarships	$2,000-$6,000	March 30

MISSOURI

Access Missouri Financial Assistance Program	$300-$2,850	April 1
Advanced Placement Incentive Grant	$500	June 1
Marguerite Ross Barnett Memorial Scholarship	$622,140	August 1

154

Minority and Underrepresented Environmental Literacy Program	$3,045	June 1
Minority Teaching Scholarship	$3,000	June 1

MONTANA

Montana Governor's Best and Brightest Merit Scholarship	$2,000	March 15
Montana Governor's Best and Brightest Merit-at-Large Scholarship	$2,000	March 15
Montana Higher Education Grant (1000 Awards given in the amount of $600,000)	$500-$600	See website
Montana Honorably Discharged Veteran Fee Waiver	Full Tuition	See website
Montana University System Honor Scholarship	Full Tuition	March 15

NEBRASKA

Roberta Marie Stretch Memorial Scholarship	$400	March 1
Ruby Paul Campaign Fund Scholarship	$100-$300	March 1
Averyl Elaine Keriakedes Memorial Scholarship	$200-$400	See website
American Legion Nebraska President's Scholarship	$200	March 1
American Legion Nebraska Auxiliary Student Aid Grant or Vocational Technical Scholarship	$200-$300	March 1

NEVADA

ABC Stores Jumpstart Scholarship	Varies	February 15
American Legion Nevada Oratorical Contest	$200-$500	January 15
American Legion Nevada Auxiliary Past Presidents Parley Nurses' Scholarship	$150	See website
American Legion Nevada Auxiliary President's Scholarship	$300	See website
William J. and Marijane E. Adams Jr. Scholarship	$3,000	See website

NEW HAMPSHIRE

Abbie Sargent Memorial Scholarship Fund	$400-$1,000	March 15
Adrienne Alix Scholarship	$1,000	March 15
Albert T. Marcoux Memorial Scholarship	$2,000	May 1
American Legion New Hampshire Boys State Scholarship	Varies	See website
American Legion New Hampshire Department Vocational Scholarship	$2,000	May1

NEW JERSEY

New Jersey Governor's Industry Vocations Scholarship	$500-$2,000	October 1
New Jersey Law Enforcement Officer Memorial Scholarship	Full Tuition	October 1
New Jersey Part-Time Tuition Aid Grant for County	$546-$1,900	June 1

Colleges

New Jersey STARS II	$2,500	June 1
New Jersey Student Tuition Assistance Reward Scholarship	$5,074,308	March 1

NEW MEXICO

New Mexico Competitive Scholarships	Varies	See website
New Mexico Legislative Lottery Scholarship	Full Tuition	See website
New Mexico Scholars Program	Full Tuition	See website
New Mexico Student Incentive Grant	$200-$2,500	See website
Paul R. Ball Scholarship	$2,000	April 21

NEW YORK

New York State Arthur O. Eve Higher Education Opportunity Program (HEOP)	Varies	See website
Caroline Kark Scholarship	Varies	April 15
Grange Denise Scholarship	$1,000	April 15
Flight 587	Full Tuition	June 30
New York State Aid for Part-Time Study Program	$2,000	See website

NORTH CAROLINA

Latino Diamante Scholarship Fund	Varies	August 15
NC Sheriff's Association Criminal Justice Scholarship	$2,000	See website
North Carolina Aubrey Lee Brooks Scholarship	$11,100	January 31
Rodney E. Powell Memorial Scholarship	$1,000	See website
North Carolina Scholarships for Children of Veterans of War	Full Tuition	See website

NORTH DAKOTA

American Legion North Dakota Oratorical Contest	$100-$400	See website
Edward O. Nelson Scholarship	$1,500	April 15
Hattie Tedrow Memorial Fund Scholarship	$2,000	April 1
American Legion North Dakota Auxiliary Past Presidents Parley Scholarship	$350	May 15
American Legion North Dakota Auxiliary Scholarships	$500	January 15

OHIO

Ohio College Opportunity Grant	$93,472,188	October 1
Ohio Safety Officers College Memorial Fund	Varies	See website
Ohio National Guard Scholarship Program	Full Tuition	See website
The Harold K. Douthit Scholarship	$1,500	May 31
Minority Scholarship (Ohio News Media Foundation)	$1,500	March 31

OKLAHOMA

Oklahoma Engineering Foundation Scholarship	$1,000	February 15
George and Donna Nigh Public Service Scholarship	$1,000	See website
Oklahoma Academic Scholars Program	$1,800-$5,500	See website
Oklahoma Future Teachers Scholarship	$500-$1,500	See website
Oklahoma Tuition Aid Grant	$1,000-$1,300	Early October

OREGON

Glenn Jackson Scholars	Varies	March 1
Ida M. Crawford Scholarship	Varies	March 1
Jackson Foundation Journalism Scholarship	Varies	March 1
Jerome B. Steinbach Scholarship	Varies	March 1
One World Scholarship Essay	Varies	March 1

PENNSYLVANIA

Pennsylvania Higher Education Assistance Agency Partnership for Access to Higher Education	$2,500	See website
Pennsylvania State Grant Program	Varies	May 1
Pennsylvania Targeted Industry Program	$500-$4,011	See website
Pennsylvania Work Study Program	Varies	October 1
Ready-to-Succeed Scholarship Program (RTSS)	$500-$2,000	See website

PUERTO RICO

American Legion Puerto Rico Auxiliary Nursing Scholarships	$250	March 15
The North Fulton Amateur Radio League Scholarship	$900	January 31
Los Padres Foundation Second Chance Program	$2,000	June 1
El Café Del Futuro Scholarship Essay Contest	$5,000	May 25
Pacific Gas & Electric Company Latino ERG Scholarship	$2,000	February 1

RHODE ISLAND

Androscoggin Amateur Radio Club Scholarship	$500-$1,000	January 31
The Byron Blanchard, N1EKV Memorial Scholarship	$500	January 31
The Dr. James L. Lawson Memorial Scholarship	$500	January 31
The New England FEMARA Scholarship	$1,000	January 31
Kent Nutrition Group, Inc. Scholarship	$1,000	February 1

SOUTH CAROLINA

Palmetto Fellows Scholarship Program	$6,700-$7,500	December 15
South Carolina Dayco Scholarship Program	Varies	See website
South Carolina HOPE Scholarships	$2,800	See website
South Carolina Federal Credit Union Annual Competition	$1,000-$4,000	March 14
South Carolina Tuition Grants	$2,500-$2,900	June 30

SOUTH DAKOTA

South Dakota Scholarship Program	Varies	February 1
Jump Start Scholarship Program	$1,866	September 1
South Dakota Annis I. Fowler Kaden Scholarship	$1,000	April 15
South Dakota Ardell Bjugstad Scholarship	$500	April 15
South Dakota Opportunity Scholarship Program	$6,500	September 1

TENNESSEE

HOPE-Aspire Award	$2,250	June 30
Hope-General Assembly Merit Scholarship	$1,500	September 1
Step-Up Scholarship	$3,500	September 1
Tennessee Dual Enrollment Grant	$1,200	September 15
Tennessee Ned McWherter Scholars Program	$6,000	February 15

TEXAS

The Chesapeake Energy Scholarship	$20,000	April 14
The Dallas Morning News Journalism Scholarship	$1,500	April 17
Dana Campbell Memorial Scholarship	$2,000	May 15
Blue Bell Scholarship	$1,000	March 1
Don't Mess With Texas Scholarship	$2,000	March 26

UTAH

American Legion Utah Auxiliary National President's Scholarship	$1,500	February 15
Animal Health International Scholarship	$1,000	February 1
Cady McDonnell Memorial Scholarship	$1,000	See website
Carl N. & Margaret Karcher Founder's Scholarship	$1,000	See website
Daniels Scholarship Program	$12,800,000	See website

VERMONT

Cumberland Farms Believe and Achieve Scholarship	$1,000	December 15
The Dr. James L. Lawson Memorial Scholarship	$500	January 31
Timothy and Palmer W. Bigelow, Jr. Scholarship	$3,000	May 31
Vermont Golf Association Scholarship	$1,000	May 1
Yankee Clipper Contest Club Youth Scholarship	$1,200	January 31

VIRGINIA

Anna Gear Junior Scholarship	$1,000	May 1
Capital One Virginia Military Dependent Scholarship	$5,000	April 30
The Gary Wagner, K3OMI, Scholarship	$1,000	January 31
Fastline Publications Scholarship	$1,000	February 1
Monty's Food Plant Company Scholarship	$1,000	February 1

WASHINGTON

Audria M. Edwards Scholarship Fund	$1,000-$10,000	May 1
Dayle and Francis Pieper Scholarship	$1,000	March 15
DPMA/PC Scholarship	$1,000	May 31
Earl Dedman Memorial Scholarship	$1,500-$2,000	May 1
Florence Lemcke Memorial Scholarship	$1,000	April 25

WEST VIRGINIA

West Virginia War Orphans Educational Assistance	Full Tuition	August 1
PROMISE Scholarship	$4,750	March 1
West Virginia Engineering, Science, and Technology Scholarship	$3,000	March 1
West Virginia Higher Education Grant	$600-$2,700	April 15
West Virginia Underwood-Smith Teacher Scholarship	$5,000	See website

WISCONSIN

I Matter Scholarships	$250-$1,000	May 30
Ladish Co. Foundation Scholarships	$2,500	May 1
Wisconsin Hearing & Visually Handicapped Student Grant	$250-$1,800	See website
Wisconsin Higher Education Grant	$250-$3,000	See website
Wisconsin Indian Student Assistance Grant	$250-$1,100	See website

WYOMING

American Legion Wyoming Oratorical Contest	$200-$500	May 15
Davis-Roberts Scholarship	$300-$1,000	June 15
MetLife Foundation Scholarship	$2,000	February 1
Rocky Mountain Coal Mining Institute Scholarship	$2,750	February 1
The Rocky Mountain Division Scholarship	$500	January 31

CONCLUSION

As a writer when you come to the moment when you realize all the days, weeks, and months that you have given to the creation of a book are soon to be behind you, you begin thinking to yourself, "How am I going to end this?" I always choose to follow the advice that I give young essayist and poets. Finish strong. Close with something you truly believe or believe in, and write about that in the most passionate and effective way you can.

A while back I was at a craft talk by the amazing writer Stephen Graham Jones, who is a Native American writer who writes novels about Native American characters...who also happen to be werewolves. His books are simply astonishing.

That day, the focus of his craft talk was on great beginnings to stories and charging young Native students to write more and how to do so. He closed his lecture by reading an essay he had just written entitled *"Letter to a Just Starting Out Native Writer—and Maybe to Myself."* This essay and his recitation of it simply floored me. (You can find it and read it yourself in the Spring 2016 Edition of Yellow Medicine Review. Yellow Medicine Review also chose to publish my essay, with which I am about to close this book.) After the craft talk, I approached him and thanked him for his words. I then immediately asked him if I could write a response to his piece, but one that focuses on speaking to young Latinx students who have a desire to write. He simply replied, "Hell yeah."

When you're reading this final part of the book, this closing essay, if you do not identify as Latinx, or Chicano, or Latina, or some variation of this identity, I hope you find Light in these words. I hope you find a way to transpose the word Latinx in your mind with the word that best describes your collective *we*, whether it be Black, or Queer, or Transgender, or whatever word you feel best describes you and people like you. I hope that you write a response to this piece offering advice to young writers who identify with your collective *we*. I hope you read and write and breathe and live and love more deeply than you did before you read this book.

I hope.

AN OPEN LETTER TO YOUNG LATINX SCHOLARS WHO DREAM OF WRITING

(And Maybe To Myself At Age 16)

Stephen Graham Jones

1. Write. Just write. Be it poem or prose, true or false. Get it out of you and onto the page. I firmly believe we would have more Latinx readers if we had more Latinx writers. You have a responsibility here, as do I, not to ourselves but to that skinny 10 year old girl from the barrio or the fields who has read 27 books from beginning to end in her short life and never loved one of them completely because she has yet to read a story that sounds like hers.

2. For every white male writer a teacher assigns you to read, find a Latinx woman writer to read as well. Don't let anyone tell you the numbers will never add up. I'll get you started with a short list here:

- *Julia Alvarez*
- *Sandra Rodriguez Barron*
- *Sandra Benitez*
- *Ana Castillo*
- *Sandra Cisneros*
- *Denise Chavez*
- *Judith Ortiz Cofer*
- *Angie Cruz*
- *Cynthia Cruz*
- *Natalie Diaz*
- *Laura Esquivel*

- *Christina Garcia*
- *Ada Limón*
- *Esmeralda Santiago*

Et cetera, et cetera, et cetera...

Estos son sólo algunos entre la multitud.
These are merely a few among the multitude.

3. You don't have to go too far off galaxies in your mind's eye for ideas for poems. Start in your grandmother's kitchen, en el jardin de su Abuelo. Listen to lover's quarrel at the taquería, watch closely as the tortillas bubble and blacken on the comal, feel your tía's hands as she returns home from the fields, or the classroom, or the office. There are poems and stories all around you just waiting to be found. Sometimes you don't even have to look for them. We are a loud people. We argue loudly. We love loudly. We live loudly. Sit in the middle of all that noise. Silence yourself, and the poem will find you.

4. In many stories they, and in some instances we, assign our characters to the role of curandera, or field worker, or maid, or gardener. And they are those things. Those things are honest and good and worthy of being written about. They should be written about. But I challenge you to remember that they are also poets, and teachers, and doctors, and senators, and dreamers, and song singers. When you are creating your characters, many times inspired by living breathing people, you must remember who you come from, who you are, and who you are destined to be.

5. When writing an essay or poem, you must know that sometimes the word for what you want to say does not exist in English. In those moments, I implore you to fall back en la lengua de sus Abuelas, the tongue of your grandmothers. *A little white cross beside the road to mark the spot where someone has tragically died,* is sixteen English words trying to say one thing, one undeniably tragic and poetic thing, but even with all those words, it still falls short. Pero la palabra in Español, but the word in Spanish... descanso...yes, that says it all perfectly.

6. It won't always be this way, but for now, many editors, many publishers, many men will see you as Brown. See you as less than. Before they see you as equal. Before they see you as anything else. Perhaps for your daughter or son it will be different, but you must know at times the fight is rigged. Unfair. But you are your mother's daughter and your father's son. If that means anything, it means this: you will fight. You will write.

You will write the wrongs of this world.

7. You come from a people who grow things from the land. Food from the earth. Food for their people. Something from nothing. Photosynthesis is a fancy word they made up to define our magic. A magic that exists in you. Remember that magic when you stare at the blank page. Remember that magic when they try to make you feel less than. You strong beautiful Latinx poets were born to rise.

8. Your strength is stronger than their ignorance.

9. Trust your voice. It took me a lifetime to learn that. Don't let it take you as long. Know that the world is ready for your voice. Your time is now. We are listening. I am listening. I am listening to every single one of you. I've grown weary of my own voice. I want to hear yours. Like you, I hope that my writing changes someone, heals them, charges them to act. But I'm too close to my own writing for it to have that affect on me. I'm waiting for your poem, your story to save me in every way a person can be saved. So speak, sing, write. Press the pencil down hard when you do. Trust me when I say, you will leave an impression on things you were not intending to impress.

10. Your heart is free. Have the courage to write from that place inside you where love resides, where beauty resides, where freedom resides. When you do, you will come to the undeniable truth that no man can ever build his wall around your voice.

ACKNOWLEDGMENTS

First and foremost, I must thank **my partner, Aida Zihuatanejo,** who inspires me every day with her art, designs, and creations. I remember coming home from work that first day as a teacher and telling her, "I quit. I'm not going back. I don't know enough. I'm cheating these students of the experience of learning. I can't do this."

It was she who calmed me and assured me that not only was I going back tomorrow, but that one day I would be an extraordinary teacher. She challenged me to get organized and to set goals. Thank you for making me go back. Like all things I write, this is for you. Always.

Thank you to **both my daughters, Aiyana and Dakota,** who both received full ride academic scholarships to attend university. I am entirely proud of both of you. Always.

I would like to thank **all of the students I have ever worked with**. Know that I learned so much from you, and know that I think of you all often. You all made me feel like a teacher. After all who could hope to be anything more than that?

Thank you to my publisher for believing in me and my vision of what I wanted this book to be. Thank you to **Sarina Cornthwaite, my proofreader** and second set of eyes. Thank you to **Iske Conradie, my editor** and third set of eyes throughout this process. Thank you Iske for your patience and for making this book look beautiful.

I've often said that high school, college, and graduate school were wonderful experiences, but everything I really need to know about life I learned in el jardin de mi Abuelo, in my grandfather's garden. I'm so grateful to **mi Abuleo** for what he taught me in the garden. It was there that I learned how to work hard, how to be proud of dirt under my fingernails, how to kneel before something and humble myself, how to pray for miracles, how to be grateful when they happened, and most importantly I learned how to help things grow. I hope I'm still helping things grow.

Lastly to **my tío Silastino**, thank you for all of the wisdom you gave me. I count you and my Abuelo among my first teachers. Your words still resonate through me. It was you who first challenged me to master words, to use them as a way out of the barrio. As a way back into the barrio to save you all. I don't know if I have, but I'm still trying.

I remember standing on the porch with you when I was nothing more than a mocoso with a curse world for the world stuck in my throat. You said to me, "Mi'jo all the best words are in English, pero all the best curse words are in Spanish." You were right. About so many things.

WORKS CITED

- *"Award-winning Essay"* by Cesar Arevalo.

- *"Award-winning Essay"* by Brittany Stinson.

- *"An Open Letter to Young Latinx Scholars Who Dream of Writing (and Maybe to Myself at Age 16) After Stephen Graham Jones"* by Joaquín Zihuatanejo originally published by Yellow Medicine Review Spring 2016 Edition.

ALSO BY JOAQUÍN ZIHUATANEJO

- *Barrio Songs*

- *Of Fire and Rain (co-authored by Natasha Carrizosa)*

- *Family Tree*

- *Like & Share*

- *Fight or Flight*

- *Arsonist*

TO BRING JOAQUÍN TO YOUR CAMPUS

for a reading or workshop contact **Gil Peña** at **gil@coolspeak.net**

ABOUT
THE AUTHOR
JOAQUÍN ZIHUATANEJO

Joaquín Zihuatanejo received his MFA in creative writing with a concentration in Poetry from the Institute of American Indian Arts in Santa Fe, New Mexico.

His work has been featured in Prairie Schooner, Sonora Review, and Huizache among other journals and anthologies. His poetry has been featured on HBO, NBC, and on NPR in *Historias* and *The National Teacher's Initiative*.

He was the winner of the Anhinga-Robert Dana Prize for Poetry. His book, *Arsonist,* was published by Anhinga Press in September of 2018, and was short-listed as a Finalist for both the Writers' League of Texas Best Book Poetry Prize and the International Latino Book Award Best Book Poetry Prize.

Joaquín has two passions in his life, his wife Aída and poetry, always in that order.

DOLLARS FOR SCHOLARS

is a walk through
scholarship essay writing,
the scholarship process,
and the transition from
high school senior to college
freshmen by World Poetry Slam
Champion and award-winning
teacher, Joaquín Zihuatanejo.

Joaquín Zihuatanejo shares his own
college scholarship story that took
him from barrio boy to award-winning
teacher and published author. Included
in Dollars for Scholars are hundreds of
scholarships that you can apply to.

ISBN 9780578616377

90000

9 780578 616377